LEAP OF FAITH

Presented by Natalie Lavelock

LEAP OF FAITH

ISBN (print): 979-8-9871926-4-1

Printed in the USA by 48 Hour Books (www.48HrBooks.com)

TABLE OF CONTENTS

FOREWORD

Moses couldn't speak…
David was too young…
Esther was a woman…
Noah was crazy…
And Jesus was just a carpenter's son… a nobody.

And yet—Moses was called to lead, David was called to be a warrior and King, Esther was called to speak boldly and save her people, Noah was called to do the impossible, and Jesus was called to save humanity.

I find it interesting that some of the greatest stories ever told happened because someone was given the opportunity to do something that challenged their belief in themselves and yet they trusted God enough to take a Leap of Faith. And when they did, miracles happened!

As entrepreneurs, we face a plethora of challenges every day. Whether it's a lack of resources, time, money, knowledge or any number of other things, there is no shortage of reasons why our businesses should not succeed. And yet, as faith-based entrepreneurs, we know that there is a God above who loves us more than we will ever know and who has called us to the work we do for a purpose greater than ourselves.

So, what do we do then when the challenge seems insurmountable? When the numbers don't add up, the dollars are too few, ideas sound crazy, and the resources become scarce— yet we know this is what we're supposed to do?

Well, let's look at just one of numerous accounts in the Bible where this actually happened and discover what we can learn about how to handle the challenges in our own lives.

This is the story of Caleb. Caleb was a leader in Israel under the direction of Moses. He was called to go inspect a land that the

Lord was sending them to inhabit. Take note of what happens during this story and consider how it might parallel some of the challenges you face as an entrepreneur.

And the Lord spoke to Moses, saying, "Send men to spy out the land of Canaan, which I am giving to the children of Israel; from each tribe of their fathers you shall send a man, every one a leader among them." –Numbers 13:1-2

Now, you can go back and read this account for yourself if you would like, but the next thirteen verses are the names of all the men who were chosen for this "secret spy" task. For the sake of your sanity (I know how it is to read all those 'begat' style paragraphs), I'm just going to tell you that Caleb was one of those men—okay? Then Moses sent them on their way to check out the land. He told them to bring back a full report of what they found—and some seasonally ripe grapes, for good measure (wink-wink). So, they went and spied out the land, grabbed some yummy produce, brought it back to Moses, Aaron and Israel, and here's what happened next…

They told Moses, "We went to the land where you sent us. It truly flows with milk and honey, and this is its fruit. Nevertheless, the people who dwell in the land are strong; the cities are fortified and very large; moreover we saw the descendants of Anak there." Then Caleb quieted the people before Moses, and said, "Let us go up at once and take possession, for we are well able to overcome it." But the men who had gone up with him said, "We are not able to go up against the people, for they are stronger than us." And they gave the children of Israel a bad report of the land which they had spied out, saying, "The land through which we have gone as spies is a land that devours its inhabitants, and all the people whom we saw in it are men of great stature. There we saw the giants (the descendants of Anak came from the giants); and we were like grasshoppers in our own sight, and so we were in their sight."—Numbers 13:27-28, 30-33

Sound familiar? You know your calling and yet it feels so far off. Perhaps there are great obstacles you will need to overcome to accomplish your task. Do you have people in your life who are like bullies—no matter how well-meaning they may be— trying to keep you from taking the ground God has told you to take? Worse yet, you must fight daily the battles of the mind. The thoughts that seek to hold you back, keep you small and sabotage your every move.

Let's continue to see what happens next...

"So, all the congregation lifted up their voices and cried, and the people wept that night. And all the children of Israel complained against Moses and Aaron, and the whole congregation said to them, "If only we had died in the land of Egypt! Or if only we had died in this wilderness! Why has the Lord brought us to this land to fall by the sword, that our wives and children should become victims? Would it not be better for us to return to Egypt?" So, they said to one another, "Let us select a leader and return to Egypt." –Numbers 14:1-4

Oh, it's getting real now! "Maybe I made a mistake." "Maybe I didn't hear God right." "Maybe I should just quit this nonsense and get a job again; at least then I'd have a steady paycheck, retirement, and insurance. Maybe things weren't so bad back when." "Why has the Lord brought me to this place of frustration and lack?" "Maybe I should just forget this and do something easier." Whining, complaining, second-guessing.

Let's keep reading...

Then Moses and Aaron fell on their faces before all the assembly of the congregation of the children of Israel. But Joshua the son of Nun and Caleb the son of Jephunneh, who were among those who had spied out the land, tore their clothes; and they spoke to all the congregation of the children of Israel, saying: "The land we passed through to spy out is an exceedingly good land. If the Lord delights in us, then He will bring us into this land and give it to us, 'a land which flows with milk and honey.' Only do not rebel against the Lord, nor fear the people of the land, for they are our bread; their protection has departed from them, and the Lord is with us. Do not fear them." And all the congregation said to stone them with stones. Now the glory of the Lord appeared in the tabernacle of meeting before all the children of

3

Israel. –Numbers 14:5-10

Ah, a last-ditch effort from the one who wants to kill your purpose—threats upon your life; either by one person, a group of people, or an assault of your own mind. Now, this may not be a literal life-or-death threat as it was for Caleb. It may look more like a shunning, withholding of resources that could help you, withdrawal of love from those you thought cared the most, of fear that you'll go bankrupt and end up dying homeless and alone. Fortunately, this is NOT how it ends for Caleb and it's NOT how it's going to end for you either.

If you chose to look this story up, you'd see in verses 11-23 that God's a bit upset by how Israel is behaving. Moses and Aaron have to do some quick talking to temper God's wrath and ultimately God decides the Israelites are going to get an extended "time-out" in the desert for disobeying Him, but that's not the part I want you to focus on. THIS is what I want you to see…

But My servant Caleb, because he has a different spirit in him and has followed Me wholeheartedly, I will bring into the land where he went, and his descendants shall inherit it. – Numbers 14:24

Did you catch that? Yes, God is perturbed that after all He has done to deliver and provide for the people of Israel; when He is about to give them His best gift yet, they are frozen in fear, refusing to do what He asks, and stepping into full-on rebellion. But despite the fear, challenges, obstacles and even the threat of death, Caleb had the courage to speak truth and take the ground God had called him to take.

That my friend, is taking a Leap of Faith.

So, what does that look like in the life of an entrepreneur? I'm so glad you asked because that's exactly what this book is all about – stories of real-life entrepreneurs who found themselves in a place where they had a decision to make. The stakes were high, and the resources were short. They decided to take their own leap of faith – and much like their predecessors in the Bible, when they got to the other side and looked back, they too saw that God had been there the whole time, standing in the gap, making a way. And my friend, He will be there for you too. That doesn't mean everything will work out perfectly the way you wanted or hoped, but He WILL be there, every step of the way – making a way because YOU are His beloved. It's time for you to take your own Leap of Faith!

Natalie Lavelock

CHAPTER 1
SAY "YES" AND LEAP

I've heard "Take a Leap of Faith" expressed in different ways. I heard, "If you reach the end of your rope, let go and let God catch you." Then I heard, "Leap and the net will appear." Another is, "Leap and you'll learn how to fly." The latest version I started saying recently, "Leap and you'll learn you had wings all along."

These all sound great, but really, how does it feel in those times that require a leap? The moments before it can be horrible. Like, really, really, uncomfortable, and sometimes accompanied by paralyzing fear. So why do it? Why leap? The moments after a leap are euphoric. The life you get after a leap is a step toward the life you've always wanted. No one has had great personal success in life without a leap.

Leaps are necessary, so let's learn how to leap. (Before I go on, here's a quick disclaimer: I'm talking about those moments in life where you really want to do something that could be amazingly great for your life and propel you forward. I'm not talking about taking unnecessary, frivolous, thrill-seeking leaps. I'm talking about the leaps that move your life forward).

I'm going to talk about how to identify when a leap is coming and needed, why it feels so daunting to leap, and the factors attempting to hold you back. I'll also talk about how to make sure you leap.

Before I go on, let me ask you a question: would you like a surefire way to know if you're on the right course in life—like you're on the right course to leap into your greatness? Would you like a compass to let you know your true North, your way to greatness? Are you sure?

Here it is: massive, massive fear.

Wait, what? Fear? Yes, fear. If you think about it, it makes perfect sense. Everything you want, that you do not currently have, is outside of your comfort zone, or outside of what you know. Therefore, attaining what's outside of your comfort zone will be UN-comfortable.

Also, your biology and wiring doesn't want you to leap. The number one job of your subconscious is to keep you alive, and it believes the way to do that is by keeping you safe, by keeping you in your comfort zone. The number one tool the subconscious uses to keep you "safe" and in your comfort zone is fear. When you're about to leap, your subconscious will turn up the fear.

Now, the fear can manifest in different ways, and it may sound like:

I don't have the money.

I don't know how.

I need to think about it.

I'm overwhelmed.

I'm not sure what to do.

It's all fear. It may feel like there's no way you can move, like you might die if you go for it; like you can't breathe, or like no one wants you around; like you're on your own, or like you should back out. Just remember, it's always a version of fear— being used by your comfort zone to keep you stuck.

Also, the bigger the leap, the more the fear. If you're going to go for something, and it's way out of your comfort zone, your subconscious is going to throw up massive walls of fear in an attempt to keep you stuck. The bigger the leap you're about to make, the more fear will try to stop you.

So, what is your true North? Fear. Want to know if you're on the right path? Fear. Do you know a leap is needed? Fear. That's your first clue if you're on the precipice of leaving your old life.

So why is a leap necessary? Because you can't tiptoe your way through massive fear. You gotta jump, or you may never take the leap.

Have you ever seen someone on the high dive at the pool or a waterfall? Have you ever seen someone scared get to the edge and wait and try to psyche themselves up, with little movements? It's so hard for them. The longer they look, the more the fear permeates their body, their legs start shaking, they look down too long, and they start to talk themselves out of it. In short, the longer one waits to leap, the bigger the chances they'll back out.

The examplitive way to do it is to make up your mind before getting to the edge, and when it's your turn, just leap. Go fast. Here's a secret to leaping: give yourself less time to think about it.

We have a saying, "Say yes and take a step." Say "Yes" in the face of your fear and take the next step... or leap. Decide to go before you're at the moment of leaping. Say yes, and when it's your turn to jump off the cliff and the way is safe, go as fast as you can.

Or sign up for the class... Or quit the job... Or send the big proposal... Take the leap. Why? On the other side of your leaps are huge rewards. Part of becoming a success in life isn't just the leap itself, it's learning to be someone who leaps.

I've leaped more times than I can count... When I was adopting my dog, I needed the money to buy enough gas to drive to where he was (about four hours away), pay the adoption fees, and buy gas for the way back. I had enough for two of the three, not all three.

Another time is when I was moving to another state to follow my dream and work for a seminar company I loved. I moved across the country, without having landed any guaranteed income from them, much less a job, and lived on my friend's couch.

Then there was the time when I was selling tickets to my first event, never having done my own event, and trusting it would turn out right.

There's the time I bought a property that cost more than we anticipated, and we were trusting we'd make the money to afford it.

Once, I bought a coaching program that cost more monthly than I was even making at the time. It was a substantial investment.

There's the time we decided to hold our events on Thursday

through Saturday, because we wanted Sunday off, when all our competitors were holding Friday through Sunday events.

Then there's the time I paid $2,500 for my first sponsorship (in this case a sponsorship is a marketing opportunity, where I could speak and offer my services).

Paying my first $20,000 sponsorship.

Hiring a team and paying more than we expected. Those leaps turned into:

A best friend who is a big part of turning my life around…

Working for that company…

Becoming a salesperson, a coach, a speaker, and then leading their events, and gaining the experience to start my own seminar company…

Getting what's become a great deal, with room for lots of family to visit, and even a mother-in-law suit for my mom to move into…

Tripling my income…

Having a life that we love and making really good sales no matter which days of the week we work, and still getting to go to church…

Making multiple five figures from that one sponsorship, which turned into multiple sponsorships and our best year in business…

Sharing the stage with some of today's top speakers and making multiple five figures in sales…

And more than doubling our income and helping a lot more people.

I pray you learn to leap.

Make up your mind before you hit the moment of the leap. Say yes in the face of your fear.

Live a life very few others can.

Leap!

Jase Souder
https://worldclassspeakeracademy.com/
success@worldclassspeakeracademy.com

CHAPTER 2
HI GOD, IT'S ME AGAIN

Hi God, it's me again.

I am at a loss and don't know what to do.

I am looking at my bank account, and I only have two months before I am completely out of money.

How did I get to zero when I once had a successful business with clients I loved?

I reflected on the path that got me here. I had slowly given up my business and had taken a job that I thought was God's path for me. It was, for a while. I needed to leave that position months earlier. I held on, determined not to leave the people I thought needed me. Then the pandemic hit, and the timing didn't feel right. I cycled through all the reasons why I stayed.

I pushed back the tears when I recalled what happened next. I lost two family members within six months. I couldn't show up for work each day in what felt like a pointless job. I needed a change.

I wrestled with building my business back up. Starting over felt impossible. I loved my business. Every day I got to help my clients achieve their goals and walk in their purpose. How can I build that back up?

I can only pray and ask God to show me what's next. I know He can and will, but doubt had created a chasm that had grown wide. It felt like an unbridgeable gap.

So, I took matters into my own hands and started looking for another job. I found one that I thought would be good, though I knew my heart wasn't in it.

I received a phone call from my son later that week. I shared the news that I was about to accept a job. My daughter-in-law joined in and said, "You shouldn't take the job; it's not who you are or what you are supposed to do." I thought about what she said, and in my heart, I couldn't disagree with her. I declined the offer the very next day. I still needed income, so I continued to search for work.

I longed to start my business, but I had so much doubt that I could make it work. I was determined to find a job that would provide for my family.

"Hi God, it's me again. I feel lost and alone. I need a sign from You that I should try to restart my business, or I will close it down for good. Please help me find what's next." I closed my eyes, not really expecting an answer.

Later, I checked my email. In my inbox was an email from the payment software I used when my business was thriving. It invited me to join a free five-day challenge to "Get the Keys to Abundance & Break Out Of Mediocrity Challenge (K.A.B.O.O.M.)" with Natalie Lavelock. I had never heard of her, but she was a Christian coach, and it was free, so why not? I signed up.

The first day of the challenge started. We were asked to write down what we joined the challenge for. I wrote, "I am standing here in the debris of my life, asking whether I should rebuild my business or walk away entirely."

I attended every day of the challenge, mostly because I had nothing else to do in between looking for work. There was an option to participate in the event at a V.I.P. level, but it cost money, which I didn't have to invest. Then I heard the topic for the bonus V.I.P. session – Emotion Mastery.

The last year had been a rollercoaster for me. I needed this. I will find the money.

I attended. I sat quietly and listened. I know that Natalie was speaking, but all I could hear were my father's words of encouragement and strength. I felt like a sponge soaking it in.

The next V.I.P. call was scheduled for a few days later. It was on sales, nothing I would need if I were closing my business. I decided to go since I had paid for it.

During that session, there was an exercise to spend 15 minutes contacting ten people about your service. I usually do what I am told, so I searched my email to see who I could reach out to.

The first contact that came up was a small Christian non-profit organization that I had from an employment search. Based on their job ad, I knew what they were looking for, so I contacted them first. I thought things like, "they can't afford me" and "this is pointless."

Honestly, they were looking for an employee, and I was pitching my service as a business. However, the point was that I completed my assignment.

At the end, Natalie presented her coaching program. It sounded fantastic but way out of my price range.

Later that day, I received a message from one of Natalie's assistants. The message said, "Natalie wanted you to listen to this song." I listened to the song. Then I listened to it again.

Here I was calling out to God, looking for answers, reaching out to Him. And here He was.

He was telling me that He was chasing after me; that He had great plans for me. He was removing my pain, and that healing had begun. The money would be there when I needed it.

It was time to say yes to building my business. It was time to help people in the way He had designed me to.

That week I also received a call from the ministry I reached out to. They became a client shortly after.

In less than six months, I was making six figures. I stopped doubting whether I should be a business owner and found clients that are a joy to work with. My life stopped being a rollercoaster and became a path forward.

Hi God, it's me again.

I was standing at the edge of a bottomless pit, a chasm that was filled with despair, depression, loneliness, heartbreak, and failure; I saw no future in sight. You replaced that gap with encouragement, laughter, friendship, and abundance. You provided a path that I could walk on.

I am so grateful for Your presence in my life. I can't wait to see what You have on the horizon for me. I know, without any doubt, that You will bridge any gap that opens before me.

Jen Wyatt
www.jenwyattmba.com
jen@jenwyattmba.com

CHAPTER 3
INTO THE WOODS

My entrepreneurial journey has been like most in many ways—a lot of ups and downs and twists and turns. Days where I wondered if I should just work at a coffee shop—the kind in the Hallmark movies. And days where I felt like I was doing exactly what I should be—living out my true purpose. But I am here to tell you I am still on the journey, and I've learned that the ups and downs are beautiful and purposeful even if it seems slow sometimes. And this Leap of Faith didn't happen in an instant; it has been a process throughout my journey.

Back before I even knew what it meant to be an entrepreneur, I got my dream job right out of school—being a therapist for a local agency. I was there for almost 20 years when I decided I wanted to learn more about coaching and treating the whole person. I went into private practice, and pretty quickly, decided to ditch the insurance model and coach women. Word of mouth and referrals in my small Midwest town seemed easy compared to the big world of online coaching. What I didn't know at the time was just how many twists and turns I would experience along the way. I thought if I put enough time and energy in, it would all just work out. I thought if I left my therapist hat in the past, I could forge on forward as a coach, never to look back. It seems like for years I have been on a journey of what I had called "Therapist to Coach." This past year, I've been experiencing some nudging to slow it down and reconsider this journey. Especially because the other parts of my business are flourishing.

Recently, I was in a session with my own wellness coach, and it all seemed to come together. We were talking about "breakthroughs" in the context of taking a Leap of Faith. This was before I knew the title of this book, which makes it even more special. Over the last year, so much had shifted, but I knew there was more to come. I could feel it, but I couldn't see it all yet. I had felt this before, but this time we were uncovering what might be holding me back.

She asked me what that would look like for me; to take this leap. As we were talking, a vision of a deep forest came to me. I could hear a breeze, I could sense a clearing up ahead, but there were still too many branches—too many barriers in my thoughts so I could not see what was on the other side. I knew I wanted to keep moving forward toward what was ahead.

I knew this particular Leap of Faith had to do with my "Therapist to Coach" quest. Memories of me consuming all I could to learn online business flooded over me. Coaching groups, DIY classes, business classes, masterminds. I have been invested and involved in so much continued learning and exploration over the last five years, it was overwhelming to think about. The feeling made me think of Grave to Gardens' song lyrics "I searched the world, but it couldn't fill me."

Throughout all this time, I was coaching. Clients would somehow find me, and referral was still working here and there. All the seeking created rich experiences and I connected with a lot of amazing people along the way. I wasn't lost in the woods. When I thought of God—thought to talk to Him about that next big decision, I could see Him there. But I pushed. Hard. And just kept committing to the "next thing." To keep with the analogy, I was wandering some. I am the type of person who has a lot of irons in the fire. So, while it was a season of deep creativity and forward movement; I was also deeply weary.

As the Holy Spirit worked, there was a feeling deep within-the calling to slow down and listen. To rest in Him. So, what did I do? I signed up for another program. I hired another coach. I hired a team. Something had to work.

One of the places I have always found peace and inspiration is the woods. I remember one day in particular, after talking with a dear pastor friend, he suggested I head out to the woods and gather up all this effort, the stressors in my personal life, and all that was not mine to carry–and give it to God. In prayer, visualizing it disappearing or carrying it off for me. It was so powerful. I went inward, to go Upward. And that is when things really started to shift. I am still coming out of the fatigue, and learning to pace myself, but I have felt great shifts. I have slowed down enough to more deeply hear the whispers of the Holy Spirit.

When I stopped pushing so hard and gave it to God, a series of thoughts, events, and opportunities started happening. I can't even describe it all here. It all started when I saw that my bariatric surgeon's team was coming to our local hospital, and I thought to myself – I should reach out to them. Then, I wondered to myself – what would it be like to take therapy clients again?

This is when things really started happening. I just shared with a friend that I was going to look into the bigger insurances, and a potential client reached out. Then another. Then the local hospital called and asked if I wanted to be on their referral list for postpartum. Then I heard about a need that is in my expertise.

At the same time, my clients happily joined my coaching membership and inquiries for my retreat spaces just came out of nowhere.

I began marveling at all the God Winks, but still had doubts. I was still feeling the ups and downs of entrepreneurship and probably focusing too much on what wasn't working. There is a balance between the creative tension of entrepreneurship and just going for it. In other words, nothing is ever perfect—and while this entrepreneurial journey is a wild ride, it is worth taking.

Remember that forest I told you about? Where I just needed to push through the branches for that next breakthrough, aka Leap of Faith? The next time I thought about that forest – I felt like something had shifted. I could see the bluff—the place I was headed for that breakthrough, that Leap of Faith. And, when I pushed through the last branch – I saw the most beautiful bridge. All along, while I was working, making decisions, planting the seeds, all the good, the bad, the ugly… God was there, taking what I was scattering about and building what I "thought" I couldn't.

He took all the love, energy, sweat, and tears and put it into building the bridge.

To say I leaped over the canyon would be a stretch, but I jumped up onto that beautiful bridge, and that is where you will find me today. From this new vantage point, I can see He filled in the gaps with opportunities, people along the way, amazing clients, wise coaching, an all-star team. And more blessings continue to be revealed to me.

Entrepreneurship itself is a huge Leap of Faith. And this year I can feel my footsteps forward even more. I am a therapist. And I am a coach. I get to be both. I get to provide whole-life wellness spaces and transformational experiences. I get to use my spaces for and with my clients. It is all coming together. I feel like this is the first chapter of the next season of my life- and this story is to be continued.

While I am so inspired by the stories where the Leap of Faith is huge, explosive, and obvious to everyone what the outcome is- and how the hero entrepreneur arrived, I believe that most leaps of faith don't look that way. Even though I know the arena of owning my own business is a wild one, I have this Leap of Faith story and a dozen others in my pocket for those rainy days. We get to experience as many Leaps of Faith and whatever happens next as often as we want. God is simply waiting for us. And, it doesn't have to be epic every time. Remember, sometimes the Leap of Faith is taking the next step forward. Then the next step. Across that next bridge, into the woods.

Thanks for listening to my story. Here is where you can find me online:

Mercedes Saurbaugh
www.intothewoods.co
Facebook Group: Her Unapologetic Life
Insta: intothewoods.experiences, intothewoods.space

CHAPTER 4
FROM GRIEF TO GRACE - A STORY OF LOSS, FAITH AND RENEWAL

I sat by my father's side in his hospice bed, observing as he whispered words that only God could comprehend. He had such a peaceful smile on his face, and I couldn't help but smile back at him.

Growing up as an only child, I had always been close to both of my parents. But watching my father's slow decline over the past five years due to Alzheimer's disease was a truly painful experience. Joseph was a man of exceptional intelligence and compassion, always speaking with purpose and intention, whether he was delivering a sermon at church or sharing his thoughts with me during a car ride. He was a deeply spiritual person, and his love for God was a central part of his life.

I inherited my father's entrepreneurial spirit and drive, and I have many fond memories of him starting various projects throughout my childhood. Despite his unconventional approach to work, Joseph was always striving for something more, and he inspired me with his ambition and unwavering determination.

However, as I sat by his bedside that Sunday afternoon, watching him slip further and further away from the world, I was overcome with a sense of loss and sadness. Why did he have to lose the most valuable part of himself – his mind – in such a cruel and devastating way?

My father passed away early the following Saturday morning, and the outpouring of emotion that filled my being as I held on to my husband for dear life was a visceral expression of my deep and profound grief. Despite the overwhelming nature of my loss, I knew that I needed to celebrate my father's life and legacy by speaking at his memorial service, both for my mother and for myself.

In the aftermath of my father's passing, I found myself navigating through a storm of emotions. The void left by his absence was palpable and I struggled to find my footing in life. Although I tried to keep busy with my business and daily activities, the feelings of emptiness and uncertainty refused to fade. It was as if a cloud of darkness had descended upon me, making it difficult to find joy and purpose in life.

For years, I struggled to find my footing, both personally and professionally. The dream of growing my business, which once brought me so much joy and fulfillment, now felt like an impossible task. I was bogged down by the weight of my responsibilities, feeling as though I was being pulled in a million different directions without any sense of direction.

However, despite my struggles, there was a small flicker of hope within me, a quiet voice urging me to reach out to the One who had always been there for me. And so, in my moment of desperation and need, I turned to God for help and guidance. It was then that I finally realized that I was not alone, that He had been there with me every step of the way, even in my darkest moments.

The Holy Spirit reminded me of the passage from Matthew 11:28-30, which had always been a source of comfort and inspiration for me. Jesus says, *"Come unto me, all ye that labour and are heavy laden, and I will give you rest. Take my yoke upon you, and learn of me; for I am meek and lowly in heart: and ye shall find rest unto your souls. For my yoke is easy, and my burden is light."*

In that moment, I realized that I had been holding onto my grief for far too long. It had become a heavy burden that was weighing me down and preventing me from moving forward in life. I understood that it was time to let go of that pain and find peace and healing. I needed to release the weight of my loss and allow myself to heal and grow. This would not be easy, but I was determined to make this change and find the peace and happiness that had eluded me for so long.

As I continued on my life's journey, I came across a truly remarkable opportunity – a complimentary call with an experienced and well-respected Online Business Strategist named Natalie, who I had the privilege of knowing for over five years. The call was filled with warmth, kindness, and an undeniable sense of God's love.

Natalie's words were like a message from the divine, filled with wisdom and guidance that left me feeling empowered and inspired. I knew in that moment that God had a special plan for my life, one that went beyond just my business and encompassed my entire being.

Motivated by this newfound sense of purpose, I made the conscious decision to nurture and strengthen my relationship with God, seeking His guidance and trust as I navigated the often-challenging world of entrepreneurship. As time moved on, I was in awe of God's abundant grace and provision. Every step of the way, I was amazed by His unwavering support and the incredible blessings He bestowed upon me.

My business has flourished beyond all expectations, experiencing remarkable growth and putting my family in the best financial position we have ever been in. We were truly blessed with a beautiful home that could only have been granted by the boundless generosity of God.

Despite facing a few obstacles and moments of uncertainty, I always remind myself of God's unwavering presence and support in my life. I recall the countless moments where He has protected me and provided for me, always walking alongside me. These memories were further solidified by the inspiring words of my father, who expressed his firm belief in me and in God's plan for my life. He wrote that God had brought me this far for a reason and had set things into motion that were beyond my comprehension. He encouraged me to have faith, to believe, and to pray with confidence and assurance.

I am truly touched by my father's unwavering faith in God and his devotion to spreading the word of the gospel. He lived a life that was filled with meaning and purpose, serving as an amazing representative of Christ. His unwavering commitment to sharing God's love and message with others was truly remarkable and inspiring.

His example has left a profound impact on me and has helped me to understand the transformative power of surrendering everything to God. Through his example, I have come to understand the power of surrendering everything to the Lord and relying on His guidance and strength. My father lived a life filled with purpose and fulfillment, serving as a remarkable ambassador for Christ, and it is his legacy that I strive to emulate.

I am constantly reminded of the importance of seeking God's direction in my life, in every decision and aspect of my existence. By following my father's lead and seeking God's grace, I am confident that I too can live a life filled with meaning and purpose, one that helps others grow in their own lives and brings glory to the Lord.

Renée Brandon
https://getsocialonpurpose.com/
hello@reneebrandon.co

CHAPTER 5
LEAP AND NEVER LOOK BACK

Early on in life, I decided that I wanted to help people. As a young child, I wasn't sure how this desire would manifest. At the age of 9, however, I knew exactly what I wanted to be: A nurse.

Unfortunately, school was hard for me. I had to study excessively if I wanted to succeed.

High school biology proved difficult for me. I had to take it twice, in fact. To add to my difficulty, my teacher was unhelpful and disliked me a great deal. He made it glaringly obvious that he didn't believe I could achieve my dream of being a nurse, primarily because of my grades. Luckily, I did end up passing, though not without a struggle.

In my senior year of high school, military recruiters came to my school to give the graduating class options after graduation. There was a moment when I seriously considered joining the military right out of high school. If I joined, I would be able to go to college for free and finally become a nurse. At the time, however, I was in a serious long-term relationship and decided to wait.

I ended up going to the community college nearby for my first year of college. In my second semester, I applied to Wayne State University for the nursing program. I remember thinking Wayne State was close enough to commute and cheap enough to afford with a full-time job. I struggled once again with the schoolwork but found tutors and steadily made my way through each semester.

After two years of undergraduate, at long last, I was accepted into the nursing program. I felt my dream was finally coming true. In my first semester of nursing school, we were required to take a Pathophysiology class. That class took everything out of me. After failing the course two times, I knew it was time to buckle down before I got kicked out of the nursing program for good. And again, I thought "I'm not going to let this beat me." I studied between classes and around my work schedule. I found tutors. Though it was a true struggle, I finally passed the third time. I will never forget the day I got my final grade for that class. I passed! The five of us that took this class three times went out to dinner and celebrated. All of us were so relieved as was my mom. Mom said she felt like she was going to nursing school with me.

As chance would have it, military recruiters came to Wayne State. I began to seriously consider the prospect. I struggled with the choice and considered dropping out since I was having a hard time working full-time and going to school full-time. Thankfully, I had a conversation with my mom. She explained to me, "You are already in the nursing program; you can always join the military later. You have no guarantees that the military will get you into another program." This conversation set the course for my future, and I decided to stick school out to the end.

During the last semester of my senior year, the military recruiters came once again and spoke to us about joining the service. I spoke with the Navy, Army, and Airforce. I seriously considered the Army and Navy. I sat on the decision for some time. It was not an easy decision. The Navy took us on a couple of trips to see what the Navy base was like and to speak to some of the other officers and ask questions. One weekend they took us to San Diego. I'll never forget the feeling of being on a Navy ship for the very first time. Exhilarated by those experiences, I knew where I was meant to be. After looking into the military three times, I finally decided to join, and I chose the Navy.

I graduated with a BSN in December 1991. I tracked down my old biology teacher and with pride announced that I graduated from nursing school. Even though he didn't have anything to say, I felt proud of my accomplishment.

Though I'd graduated, I still needed to pass the NCLEX exam. In nursing school, the NCLEX was widely feared, and professors made every effort to stress the importance of the exam. Most college students celebrate on graduation day, but for a nurse, graduation day is basically just another day. The dreaded NCLEX exam still awaits. And everyone knows, you're not really a nurse until you pass that bad boy! This test is what would definitively make me a true nurse. If I passed, I would officially become an RN. At this time in February 1992, you could only take the exam twice a year, in February and August. If you failed the test, you had to wait until the next testing period.

I didn't come all this way to fail at the end! There was no way I was letting those teachers who said I'd never make it win. I was going to pass that test! So, I took not one, but three NCLEX prep courses. I studied day and night to make sure I was ready. I was determined I was passing this test.

And as if something felt my resolve needed to be tested one more time, a snowstorm blew through Detroit while my prep classes were taking place. Not only was the test given only twice a year, but you also had to be right on time or risk being kicked out of the testing room. These people don't mess around! If I missed this, I would have to wait until August. I wasn't going to let the snow stop me from taking this test and becoming a nurse. I booked a hotel across the street from the testing building along with some nursing friends. At long last, I took the NCLEX exam in February of 1992.

While I was waiting for the exam results, I was really struggling with whether to join the Navy or to stay in Michigan. Even though I made my decision to join the Navy, I was terribly scared to move away from home for the first time.

I can look back and honestly, say the next decision I made was the most important of my life. I decided to take the leap and do it. As I was standing there, signing the enlistment papers I felt excited about my next adventure. I knew this was what I was supposed to do.

My biggest fear was looking back and thinking, 'I wish I would have…"

I believe this sentiment is ever important. I didn't want to ever look back and wish I had done something. Over the years I have lived by these words and have given high school graduates the same advice.

Two months later I received a big envelope in the mail. I couldn't believe my eyes. I honestly think I was a little in shock. I opened the envelope and started to cry. I called my mom crying. "Mom, I passed!" I passed the NCLEX exam on the first try. And there it was... proof that dreams do come true. Proof that hard work pays off. Proof that when you commit to doing something and go for it with all your heart, you can do anything!

My next leap of faith came at the end of June when I left for Officer Indoctrination School for 6-weeks of training. After graduating from OIS, I went back home to spend time with my mom before leaving. I drove to CA with my sister, my clothes, and my car to start my new journey as an officer in the military. I still remember that overwhelming feeling I had when I put my sister on the plane back to Michigan. I was alone for the first time in my life, and I will remember that moment of loneliness for as long as I live. That loneliness was powerful. I remember thinking "What have I done?" I was more than 2,000 miles from home and didn't know anyone, but it was time to take that leap of faith. I took charge of my life. Despite my instructor's lack of faith in me, I graduated from nursing school. Despite my doubts about the military, I put my all into it.

I took that leap of faith, and I never looked back.

Samantha Rawlinson, RN
Samantharawlinson.co
Samantha@Samantharawlinson.com

CHAPTER 6
WORK + PRAYER + FAITH = VICTORY

Retirement is bliss!... or so it is said. But like most things our work is never done. Well maybe our secular version is but is our God work ever done?

As my retirement from public education began, at the age of 51 (young I know), the number one question I was asked was, "Now what are you going to do?" As I pondered this question for several months, I looked at my "short" list of to do's which wasn't going to take too long to complete. Looking at the "longer" to do list I really didn't have an answer to that question, I hadn't really started that list (except to be at home). Sure, staying at home full-time was an option; so was a host of other things, but nothing was resonating with me. My own question was: "Why does everyone think I need to continue to work? I am young,-yes, but I earned this retirement for a reason, right? To be retired."

As the summer faded and fall began, I tackled my "to-do" list and enjoyed my family time and first Christmas as a retired citizen. Life was good! A resounding question seemed very urgent though from many of my schoolteacher friends and former colleagues who were asking, "Will you sub for me?" So, in January I began to substitute teach at local schools. Oh, how I missed being around students! I love aiding them, helping them figure out a problem or issue and seeing that "light bulb" switch on when they learn something new, smiles when you say hello to them in the hallway, being there for teachers and other personnel as they need an extra helping hand or a shoulder to lean on. It just felt good to be around people daily.

Then there were my homeschooling friends calling to ask for my help, guidance, and advice in coaching their children.

Homeschool families sometimes feel they are left with very few resources offered to them locally, such as academic, career and personal counseling. They were calling me as a trusted friend, colleague, or teacher/counselor because they had worked with me before or had been referred to me. Most of their questions were centered around school and career counseling issues or what their student wants to do beyond high school. This gave me a sense of still being needed in my expertise.

"MY" answer to "MY" question of retirement was that I "really wanted to just be retired". But—something kept telling me that "work" wasn't done yet. As I began to really focus on God and His plan for me, I asked Him— "God what am I supposed to do?" Then one Sunday in church, while singing a congregational hymn, God delivered His message to me in song— "We'll work 'til Jesus comes." What? Ummm… when is that supposed to be? Oh right, "We do not know the hour" (Luke 12:40). OH, how this song spoke to me—my GOD WORK as a Christian was not even close to being done!

At this point, I really dove into my Bible study (Discerning the Voice of God by Priscilla Shirer), one that I had started two times before but had never finished and finished it. I realized that I never finished it because it wasn't God's timing for me to do so– until then! In His time, not mine (so easy to forget we are not in control). As I studied and began to really listen for "my calling," I realized that the Great Commission was my job, always had been and always will be while on this earth! As Christians, we ALL have been given this task but too often we push it aside. Don't get me wrong, it's in the back of our minds but only comes out a couple times a year when we "do our part," "our duties" such as helping with Vacation Bible School, church camp, Easter programs, Christmas programs, etc. whatever we make time for. But He gave us talents, gifts, TOOLS that we are to use to build His ETERNAL Kingdom by helping and sharing Him and the Bible with others! We are to bring in His sheep; the non-Christians, CLOSET Christians, He wants us to bring Him the people!

Besides raising my own children (once a mom always a mom) and 28 years in public education, teaching Missouri's youth to be contributing members of society, my most important work wasn't finished. A Christian never retires from God's work!

With that I prayed, took a Leap of Faith, joined with a Christian Business Coach and Consultant – Natalie Lavelock. Coaching, and started training with Natalie; plus the Bible book study and learning from Discerning the Voice of God (Shirer) has continued the steppingstone path of life of retirement from my secular jobs onto my new path that lay at my feet; with ALL the gaps being filled by God's design. Ta-Da–Melissa Eiserer, Career Coaching and Consulting was born!

Ephesians 2:10 (NIV) says *"For we are God's handiwork, created in Christ Jesus to do good works, which God prepared in advance for us to do."* He prepared me in advance to do His work. I've been doing it all along but selfishly thought it was the end. Nope! We'll work 'til Jesus comes...

A wise woman once told me as I was walking out the back door to put my suitcase in the car and head off to college, "Melissa, look out for yourself because no one else will." This woman was my beautiful, God-fearing, Jesus-loving momma. Yes, she knew God had my back. But she was reminding me that I needed to be wise in my decisions and listen to my inner voice, the Holy Spirit, to guide me along the way. Momma was also a beautiful piano player at home and in the church. The love of old hymns and scripture she and my father (played the guitar) instilled in me has brought peace so many times in life. When I really sing out and reflect on those scripture-based hymns, that's where I find clarity through God's words so much of the time. This time was no different. My life is taking on a new shape in Faith-based coaching. I'll work until Christ comes again doing His work as He lays it out in front of me.

My prayer is that God uses me and my talents as a Christian Faith-Based Coach to enrich the lives of the families, students, parents, and clients that have been entrusted to me. That with Gods leadership, I serve with passion to assist everyone to find their purpose in life. That He blesses all who have walked with me along the way; He knows I could never repay them for giving of their time, advice, coaching and guidance in my life calling. That my work be done for His glory! (In Christ's name, amen.)

I am blessed, grateful, and appreciate all God has provided in my life. Time will take one day at a time, using sweet hours of prayer to fill in the gaps while I work 'til Jesus comes. As I continue to fully discern God's voice and seek Him, I will forever be reminded that my reward for having faith is VICTORY, victory in life eternal through Jesus Christ.

The work we do matters because it is a way for us to glorify God and serve others.

"For we are God's fellow workers. You are God's field, God's building." –1 Corinthians 3:9 (NIV)

Work + Prayer + Faith = VICTORY

Melissa Eiserer
Email: melissa@melissaeiserer.com
Facebook: Melissa Eiserer, Career Coaching & Consulting

CHAPTER 7
THE VOICE OF GOD

"*You need to call John.*"
"*You need to call John.*"
"What?"
"*You need to call John.*"

It was January of 2016. Every time I would sit down to do my devotions, I would hear the still, small of God whisper, "*You need to call John.*" And every time I would ignore it until about three weeks later. While I was doing my devotions one Saturday morning, the voice was so strong, I felt the Lord shaking me and saying, "*When are you going to listen to me and call John?*" So, I proceeded to get up out of my chair and started walking towards the kitchen to get our church directory to call John. Wait.

Then I paused, and I said "Lord, am I really hearing you tell me to call John?" This is crazy. I am President and CEO of my company, we are just getting ready to acquire another company, and you want me to call John. Really?

So, like Gideon in the bible, I laid down my fleece and I said, "If that's really what you're calling me to do… if John is in church tomorrow, I will talk with him."

I previously worked with John years before as a cardiology nurse and assistant director in the cardiology department when he was CEO of our local community hospital. He was now COO of the much larger health system that had acquired our hospital a few years before.

You see, I was pretty sure John wouldn't be in church the next day because he usually wasn't. He would attend once every five to six weeks or so due to his position as the COO of our large health system and having grown children living out of the area. If John

31

wasn't working, he was visiting his family. The odds were in my favor... or so I thought.

There I was sitting in the choir loft at church the next day and forgetting that I laid out my fleece the day before until... I looked out into the congregation and there was John, with his wife, in church. What? Really, Lord? And to make matters worse, the sermon was about listening to the voice of God and His call on your life. Well okay, Lord, hit me with a 2X4, why don't you!?!

I had secretly hoped that by the time it took me to get out of the choir room and back into the sanctuary, John would be gone. He was still there, so, I took a deep breath, approached him, and said, "John, could I meet with you sometime this week?" He said, "Sure, give Marian a call." Marian was John's executive assistant. So, I did. The meeting was scheduled for Thursday.

There I was, sitting in John's office, being obedient.

He says, "Hi Michele, what can I do for you?"

"Hi John, I have no idea why I am here. I just know the Lord told me to talk with you, so here I am."

We both laugh and he says, "Well, with your nursing, business, and management background, we would love to have you back. Let me have you talk with Carrie."

Carrie was the new President of our local hospital, and I had just met her a few weeks prior at the annual chamber dinner of which I was President. She was delighted. We met.

Long story short, I took a Leap of Faith and became Sr. Practice Manager in the East over four practices with twenty-six employees and six doctors within the health system. Unfortunately, it was not with Carrie. I inherited disgruntled employees who hated my bosses and that is putting it mildly. I was hired for change management and manage I did. What seemed like a dream job soon became a nightmare.

My first clue should have been when one of the nurse practitioners pulled me aside prior to taking the position and said, "Don't do it. You are walking into a disaster." I didn't listen. I was listening to God. And how do you say no to God? He was calling me, and they needed me for such a time as this.

I began working day and night, night and day. I was getting less than four hours of sleep a night. There was so much to do, and we were implementing a new electronic healthcare record for the health system and the East was implementing it first. We were the guinea pigs.

As Vince watched this job drain the life out of me, he began to question if I had really heard the voice of God. It got so bad he started looking for other positions for me within the health system. He found one and he said, "You would be perfect for this."

To which I replied, "If the Lord wants me to have it, it will happen. He must have me here for a reason."

The following Friday, my boss meets with me and says, "I don't know how to say this, I'm not sure I want to say this, I don't what to lose you, however, there is a brand-new position within the health system that you would be perfect for, and I need to let you know about it. What are you going to do?"

To which I replied, "I'm going to apply." I did. It was the same position that Vince found.

I interviewed and was offered the position. It meant a cut in pay. I wasn't sure if I should take it or not, so I prayed about it and heard the Lord say, "Take it, it will be okay." It was. My new boss had already gone to human resources and asked them to match my current pay. I loved my new job and I got to work with my previous boss as well.

Eventually, I became the Employer Health Consultant. I loved working with employers to create a healthier workforce.

Then COVID-19 happened, and everyone's world turned upside down, including mine. Three things happened at the beginning that would change my world forever.

The jobs I loved became all about COVID-19 and helping employers navigate the ever-changing rules. Instead of being out and about, I was stuck at home like everyone else. Our managed print and IT business tanked. No one was printing. Even though we were considered essential, most of the businesses we worked with weren't.

Our son and daughter-in-law moved to Denver, Colorado and

took our adorable little granddaughters who were four and almost two at the time. Our daughter still lived near us but couldn't visit.

I met a publicist.

In January of 2020, just before COVID was a thing, Vince & I traveled to a conference for the company we owned. While there, after every session, we needed to switch tables. Three consecutive times, we sat at a different table with the same woman. Then, as we were walking to a session after lunch, who did we meet? The same woman. So, I said, "For some reason the Lord wants us to meet. What is your name, and what do you do?"

"I am Suzy, I publish itty-bitty books."

Really? Hmm…

For years I have heard the Lord calling me to write a book on aging well. I respond with, "I don't know how." And that was the end of that, or so I thought. In comes Suzy and COVID. I was stuck at home instead of going to networking events. My "new" excuse of not having time was eliminated. My distraction of my two little granddaughters was eliminated. ELIMATED! I started writing… actually, I started staring at the blank pages. Nothing. I had so much to share, I had the template. I had the time. But I didn't know where to start. Several months went by. Still nothing!

I prayed, and prayed, and prayed. Lord, help me! Did I really hear you? Then the words started, they flowed, and in the end, I had too much information. I had to keep condensing. After all, it's an itty-bitty book. I didn't want another book you read and then put on a shelf never to be read again. I wanted it to be a reference.

It was finally finished and became a bestseller in July of 2021. I asked God, now what do I do with that? And God answered.

In October of 2021, I left my hospital position and started an online business helping women uncover their 'why' beneath their weight to become happier, healthier, and feel like a hottie through FREEDOM weight loss.

My son and daughter-in-law had been asking us to move to Colorado with them. So, we did. We sold our business and our house in 2022. We moved to Colorado. Now I get to be with my granddaughters, live my passion, travel, and work from anywhere.

What did I learn? Listen, and when God whispers, you say "YES" and take a Leap of Faith!

Michele McHenry, RN, MBA
www.michelemchenry.com
michele@michelemchenry.com

CHAPTER 8
BETRAYED, BROKEN AND BLESSED - HOW LOSING MY FAITH HELPED ME FIND MY PURPOSE

January 10, 2019, became my last gratitude journal entry. Why? Because on January 11, 2019, everything in my life came crashing down. I was working on a project for my business when I got a call from my mom. I will never forget those words, "I just got off the phone with my doctor; I have cancer." Those three words destroyed every part of my being in one split second. I truly don't know how to describe how I felt other than my mind went blank, and my body went numb. The fear was overwhelming. It shattered me into a million broken pieces. I've been through a lot, but nothing ever broke me like that. Ripping out my soul would have been less painful.

I never knew it was humanly possible to cry for so many hours straight. My eyes were nearly swollen shut. The tears burned my skin so badly I couldn't wash my face. Crawling into bed that night, I glanced at the nightstand and saw my gratitude journal. I was never so angry in my life. I picked up my journal and said, "What good is this – it's nothing but a piece of garbage," and threw it in the drawer. I never touched it again.

I felt so betrayed. By life, the universe, and yes, even God. All I had were questions with no answers. The negative rhetoric poisoned my mind. Has it spread? How long will she live? What if the treatment doesn't work? Will she even survive the chemo? What will I do without my mom? At that moment, faith and gratitude became meaningless terms.

Nothing mattered to me anymore, including my business. I realized that success didn't matter if my mom wouldn't be there to see it. I lost my faith in everything and never felt so alone. Up until that point, I was surviving on faith. Faith in God, angels, spirit… and in an instant, it was gone. How could I have faith in any entity that could allow this to happen? I thought to myself; I must have been stupid to believe in something that I can't see, feel or hear. So, in addition to reeling from my mom's diagnosis, I was grieving the loss of my faith.

Those first few months were the worst. Navigating the relentless tests, never-ending doctor's visits, surgeries, wrong staging, and astronomical medication costs— I was barely functioning. I was living in a state of fear to the point where I was physically, emotionally, and mentally numb all of the time. My business was at a standstill, and I was making bad decisions – one that almost cost me years of work. And sadly, I didn't care. But eventually, once the testing was done and they determined the correct staging, things started to turn a little bit for the better. The prognosis, while not wonderful, was encouraging. Although the final determination was Stage 4, there was an unexpected blessing attached to this. Due to the type of cancer and staging, the treatment plan did not include chemo. I never felt good about her going through chemo, so despite the staging, I felt oddly relieved. And, even more crazy, so did she.

The treatment would allow her to continue with her daily routine without too much disruption, and there was hope for remission. When I heard the doctor say that remission was possible, it was the first time in months that I could feel a twinge of faith coming back.

I have learned many life lessons from this experience, some of which I could do without. But one that stood out the most was that I needed to be broken to become the person I wanted to be. Three weeks before my mom's diagnosis, I was speaking to a coach about my stubborn success blocks and the many walls I had built around myself. I quipped; "It would be easier to break into Fort Knox than penetrate my cement prison."

He asked me how I was going to break through them.

I said, "I don't know." And I meant it. I didn't know.

Well, God took care of that one because those walls were shattered just a few weeks later. And all it took were three words: "I have cancer." I don't believe anything else could have penetrated those cement walls. But they needed to come down. And I'm guessing that God knew that.

Picking up those shattered pieces and facing the demons hidden behind them wasn't easy, and it often felt like I was pouring salt on a wound. Managing my emotions around my mom's illness and my newfound vulnerabilities was a bit much. I knew I needed help.

For some reason, I thought of the book that first introduced me to using a gratitude journal. I read it again but still wasn't keen on restarting my writing practice. However, I reflected on my positive experiences before my mom's diagnosis, and I wondered... could I have gotten angry at my gratitude journal in vain? And more importantly, could I have gotten angry at God in vain?

As the dark cloud around my life started to lift, the emerging light helped me see two precious gifts hiding in plain sight. First, I recognized that I wouldn't take any meaningful leaps of faith in my life unless I was pushed off the cliff by something that wasn't in my control. I had to learn to navigate a different kind of chaos to prepare me for what would come. Although I didn't like how any of that felt, I needed to go through it. The second was that although my mom's diagnosis wasn't good, there was hope in her prognosis.

So, I thought, hmmm... maybe my gratitude practice was working all along—I just couldn't see it through the fear and pain. And perhaps God, the angels, and spirit were always by my side helping me navigate the chaos. Still toying with those ideas, I reluctantly followed the author's advice and started a new journal.

As I practiced gratitude for even the smallest blessings, the divine light of God's grace was helping to heal my heart. Ideas, inspiration, and thankfully, hope started to slowly creep back into my life. I knew it was time to stop hiding and playing things safe because life is too short and there are no guarantees. You can't wait for someday to live your dream – today is the only someday you have.

I was finally ready to take a significant leap of faith and pivot my business to align with my soul's purpose. The mission I had envisioned for my life's work started to matter again. Even better, my mom's tests showed that her treatments were moving in the right direction— I knew in my heart this was a gift from God. Dare I say, healing started to happen for both of us.

A life-changing blessing that came from this experience was that it reminded me how important it is for lightworkers to share their gifts with the world. During this troubling time when I needed help, the first thing that came to my mind was to revisit a book that helped me in the past.

This made me realize that books are often one of the first places people turn to for help when they are going through a challenging period. Many times, books are the first line of defense in healing. Things in my life didn't change until I picked up that book for the second time. It inspired me to take the small actions and mindset shifts that jumpstarted the healing process. The author of that book was a stranger to me, yet her words of wisdom helped me make the changes I needed to start healing. The power of words was never more evident.

This was my big lightbulb moment, and my mission became clear. I decided to help lightworkers find their story and turn their wisdom into a transformational book that changes lives. Finally, after almost two decades of searching, I found my true purpose. And wouldn't you know it? As soon as I decided to pivot in this new direction, I came across the perfect name for my business. That became the beginning of my new journey to help make this world a better place, one book at a time.

It's been four years since that fateful day, and I still struggle. But I know God has always been there, guiding me through times of darkness and light. I may not understand his plan, but I know he has one. So, I now trust that whatever I am handed is given to me for a reason. And for that, I am genuinely grateful.

Michelle Bybel
writeintention.com
info@writeintention.com

CHAPTER 9
MY FRYING PAN MOMENT

For as long as I can remember I have been in search of meaning, my purpose. Reading book after book hoping one of them would tell me what I was meant for but never finding an answer. I grew up in the church, and I came from a good home with parents who loved me, but I always seemed to be lost. Wondering why everyone else seemed to have it all and I was just waiting for life to begin.

At a time in my life when I was at my lowest, I found myself free from an abusive partner but alone with two small children. Still searching for a path forward, I saw an ad in my local paper about finding your purpose. I called and attended my first ever session on being a life coach.

Sitting in that room, I was amazed by these people who all seemed to glow with passion talking about what they wanted from their life. I remember thinking, I want what they have. I started researching, reading, and attending every lecturer who came to town, and I became fully immersed in learning and the "new age" practices and ideologies. I found myself being one with God, connected to the entire universe. A universe where everyone "joined" back to God once they learned what they were meant to do in this life.

My heart was crying out to help people like me who were lost and needed a path. But the practicality of it all was, I had two small children, and I needed to provide for them. Not ready to risk the stability they needed, I went to school and became a CPA. I entered the workforce and moved up the ranks into executive management, leading teams, special projects and eventually departments, still never feeling quite fulfilled.

Still fully immersed in the new age, I was studying the mind, thoughts, and manifesting. I shared with my friends and anyone who would listen about the law of attraction and how people were using it to manifest anything they wanted. I read book after book trying to find the secret of how it worked, because I just could not get it to work for me.

My feelings of not being good enough, or life is meant for other people not for me, still played in the background of my life and at times would pull me back into sadness or depression. This is when I would pull back from life. I would hide inside my "busy," so people didn't see the hurt and pain that I was really in.

In 2010 I married my husband; we had two more children, and life was good. Still feeling life was meant to be more, and being financially secure, I decided it was time to explore the world of Speaking and Coaching. I went from program to program and certification to certification, learning and practicing in my own life and helping employees and my private business clients. I seemed to have a knack for listening to people who were hurting and stuck. I knew how to help them find comfort and direction and encouraged them to move forward in their business or life. While this made my heart happy, I still felt lost. Still looking for purpose and direction. Still waiting for my life to start.

In January 2021, I started yet another coaching program that promised purpose and fulfillment. This time I was going to find my voice and launch my Speaking and Coaching business. I began with excitement and determination that this would be the one that worked. One of the lessons was on spirituality and needing to be grounded in faith. The coach suggested that we read either "The Buddha Within" or "The Kingdom Principles."

I thought I already had that area of my life covered, but since I was still searching, I downloaded "The Kingdom Principles" by Dr. Myles Monroe. I listened to it three times, and each time I had more questions. My sister was always praying, talking about God, and telling me all these stories of things that had happened to people, so she became my main source of information. I asked, she answered. She invited me to an online program at her church called Alpha; she told me that I would find the answers I was looking for.

On one of our Wednesday night meetings a leader asked me what I hoped to get out of this program, and my answer was very definite.

"I want God to come down, stand in front of me, hit me over the head with a frying pan, and tell me what it is I am supposed to be doing with my life."

It caused a little chuckle and another question: "Do you have options?"

I did. "Do I continue working on launching my own business and ignoring my family or do I just keep working and come home and color with my kids?"

After years of not finding my path on my entrepreneurial journey and not seeing a result, I was tired and ready to give up. A few months earlier at my job I was asked to take over the Human Resources department. I used my coaching to develop people, teams and processes and thought that would be good enough. Maybe I could find fulfillment, and if I didn't, well then maybe this was all life was meant to be. Being a wife, mother and nana should be enough. I was ready to quit dreaming of having my own business and the lifestyle that came with it.

So... Do I keep going in my business or quit? This was the first time I posed the question out loud, not expecting an answer but at the point where I was ready to quit.

The next morning, I went down to my home office. I had been working at home for over a month now because I had covid and then vertigo. My work wanted me back in the office, but I was just not able to drive or walk very well. I also really enjoyed working from home. I was there to send my kids to school and there when they came home. It was the freedom I'd been working towards for years.

As I was fully engrossed in a large spreadsheet that I was not enjoying but needed to be done, my boss messaged me requesting a meeting. I called him at 11 AM as scheduled and found myself unemployed. There was an unexpected blessing: I was given a severance that was nearly six months' worth of my salary. I closed my company computer and sat in silence for about 10 minutes.

I was stunned and happy, overwhelmed and at peace all at once. I called my husband to share the news. After a shared moment of disbelief and joy, he pointed out that now I would have the time I needed to build my business. Frying pan received.

Then I opened my laptop with a new hope and said, "OK, God, what is it I am supposed to do now?" That is when I came upon a faith-based coaching program. Over the next couple of months, I would be exposed to a wonderful group of people who were advancing God's Kingdom in or through their business. I now have a thriving business where I work with Kingdom Women Entrepreneurs who want to thrive in their own business.

God told me that my purpose, everyone's purpose, is to advance His Kingdom. The desires He put on my heart are to Speak and Coach women, to raise up Kingdom Women to advance His Kingdom on earth as it is in heaven. To raise up powerful women warriors who know they were born to influence, to know the Truth of who He says they are, and to defeat the enemy in their own lives so that they can live a significant life.

There was a moment where the shame of my time in the new age overcame me; how could God forgive me for believing in the lie? He does. God assures me that nothing is wasted, and it's true, everything I learned and studied has contributed to who I am in my business.

I realized that during my prodigal return I was in the world looking for my identity when it was with God the whole time. I realized all the time that God was with me protecting, providing, and placing the path before me.

There were moments in my life where I remember asking "is this my life I'm living"? I took a Leap of Faith and God was there waiting. I am now living a life with balance and fulfillment working every day helping women overcome fear and overwhelm to powerfully stand up in who God says they are. I now wake up every day saying, "I'm born for this."

Christine Locke
christine@womanofinfluence.ca

CHAPTER 10
FOLLOW YOUR CALLING

In my life, I have had many encounters with Jesus. I would like to share with you a series of events. Thus, becoming an outstanding Leap of Faith.

Back in 1989, we were in our tenth year of marriage, with two young sons. Busy lives as families who have small children are.

I also worked in our local church.

One day, the pastor asked to meet me. He said a notification came about a seminar. Praying, he sensed God saying for me to attend.

It is not only to help your own church, but likewise for other churches.

It intrigued me and scared me. After a lot of prayer, I decided yes, I would do it.

Soon afterwards, my husband told me he wanted out of our marriage. Shocking me. Not having any idea, he was unhappy.

I stopped the positions that I worked. Then I found myself looking for a good paying job.

After counseling and a six-week separation, we got back together. I got a position with USPS as a letter carrier.

Years went by. My son entered junior high. He joined the youth group at a new church.

A bible study became available which I attended. Through this study we learned, we all come to a crisis of faith.

In a crisis of faith, we find ourselves at a crossroads. Encountering a crisis of faith, you face it by taking a leap of faith.

Which path will you take?

I recognized all those years ago that I had stepped away from the direction God was leading me.

So, I made a recommitment to God. I told Him I was not going to let anything interfere again.

You guessed it, the blockage came again.

My husband became ill. The doctor said he only had a 30% chance of living.

Living, he could be in a coma. If he wakes up, he will have a different personality. Again, feeling overwhelmed and devastated, but this time I remembered my commitment to God.

After a few days in a coma, he woke up. He experienced memory deficiencies and difficulty controlling his emotions. His anger became scary. As time went by, I got several positions in the church. Moving forward with God along with caring for my family.

One day, the pastor called me to his office. He shared with me a seminar that was coming soon. After praying, he perceived God saying that I should go to it.

Again, being led to this conference. I went. It. Was. I obtained countless breakthroughs. I couldn't wait to share it with others.

Time went by. Then it got worse at home, I made the hard decision to leave this time. I stepped away from my duties, again. I did not tell my situation to many, but some I did.

During our time of separation, I worshiped elsewhere. I felt members of the old church turned against me.

After medicine and counseling, the scary anger disappeared.

We got back together.

After a while, I did not feel that I was fulfilling something in my life. I sensed that God was leading me to write.

This was hard, because I was told all my life that I had no talent for writing. That I should never even get a job as a secretary. No one would understand me.

However, the idea thrilled me, and I wanted to prove them wrong. So, I moved forward with writing, and I became excited.

Then one day, I sensed from God that He wanted me to go back to work. I argued with Him. I knew what He meant. Agreeing, I asked which church. I was even willing to go back to the old one if He made that clear.

That week, the new directory of the old church came out. I found my youngest and my name not in it. As I had worked there, the only way to remove the name of a person was if they asked to be removed or passed away.

Realizing I was not imagining the rejection, this hurt even deeper. After basking in that pain for a short time, I came to realize God gave me my answer about which place to work.

One Sunday, the new church was doing a recruiting for the children's program. I tried to escape through the front door (still being argumentative). A sweet elderly lady grabbed my hands, telling me to go back in. I was good at what I did, I should go back.

It shocked me and I took a step backward. I hadn't shared my previous work with anyone. I was hiding. But you cannot hide from God.

My husband and I tried to walk to our car, but my feet felt like they were walking in quicksand.

I shared with my husband that I had to go back. He agreed with a gleam in his eye and a little chuckle.

I walked back in and asked for Jane. I found her and asked her to sign me up. She proceeded to ask me questions. All I kept hearing from her was the word "you" in her questions.

I shared with her that God told me to go back to work. This is not about me and what I want, it is what I feel God wants. I said to place me in her hardest position, and I'd do it. Even how often needed I will do it out.

She paused and then asked if I had taught. I smiled and proceeded to give her a brief verbal resume of what I did.

She placed me in the preteen program. We went to lunch the following day. She shared her dreams with the preteens, and I shared my past: the separation, everything. I did not want to experience what I had before.

I worked for about two Sunday services and my next schedule was on Saturday night. Being an experiential teacher, I like to experience what we are learning. That week it was in diversity. So, I went to Trader Joe's and bought all those frozen dishes from around the world.

All week I requested to have my eight-hour day on Saturday. We only had one eight-hour day a week. Saturday morning came. My boss told me I am now required to work ten hours. I reminded him of what I had requested all week.

I am not sure what he said to me, but all I heard was, is it me or money? Working at the post office was security for me, just in case I went through again what I did all those years before.

As my boss talked, my reply even shocked me. I told him that I have many things in my life that are far more important to me and that I might need to resign. This time it was his turn to be shocked.

Later, he came to me and said he had worked it out. I didn't need to work ten hours and, to my relief, was able to teach after all.

The kids and adults loved all the food, and we discussed the differences in food from different countries. We like some, then some we don't. But the food is still good.

When I got home, my husband and I discussed it. With the agreement, we decided for me to leave the post office. We both recognized the right thing for me to do. Put God first. My husband reassured me not to worry about the money.

On Monday, I submitted my two-week notice.

About two weeks later, my husband's work realized they had not been giving him his raises. He received $500 more a month.

My niece moved in while going to college and gave $200. The church hired me as Preteen Leader.

We got enough money to cover everything. I took a Leap of Faith moving forward. By doing so, I helped and mentored over 600-700 kids and their parents.

After I started, the class grew from three to around twelve. After that Saturday class, it went from 12-75 within two more weeks.

Along the way, I started mentoring women. I felt God was leading me to do it online. After a very clear sermon on mentoring, I knew I was on the right track.

If I did not move toward God and took the Leap of Faith in my crisis of faith. I would not be doing what I am doing today. I would not have helped so many people. Take that Leap, it is so worth it.

Linda Jo Jenkins
Lindajojenkins.com
707-479-1812

CHAPTER 11
TRUST THE KNOWING

In the summer of 2014, my life fell apart. Of course, it began invisibly much sooner, but the unraveling of a life built over the previous 12 years finally became visible to the naked eye in late July.

As I said goodbye to my husband, my home, and even my dog, I whispered a wary hello to a new reality. Why was it all happening so fast? I didn't know, but something inside me did.

Summer became fall and big questions loomed: Where did my life go? What do I want now? Who am I? Did I cause this by asking for more from my life?

I was quite unsure where all this change would lead me until a phone call came out of the blue offering some direction.

"We found you through LinkedIn," I heard a voice on the line, "We're looking for a fitness and nutrition expert for our website – we need a female counterpart to our male guru."

After years of working in fitness and developing my own approach to nutrition and exercise, I felt confident that I could do this "expert" thing. My only insecurity? I was clueless about online stuff.

Though I had a profile, I didn't understand how LinkedIn worked. Still, something in my gut told me to go for it, so I submitted the requested interview video, I got the gig and was introduced to a whole new world I had intentionally steered clear of...

The internet.

The pressure to perform was immense from day one. I felt as lost as if I had moved to China without taking time to learn the language. Though I had a team in place to help me with every little detail, I still felt embarrassed by what I didn't know. They assured me they would do all the work behind the scenes; I just had to be the face and voice they wanted.

It took a few months for me to realize the persona they wanted me to portray clashed terribly with who I am. They wanted clicks and quick-fix programs to bring in revenue, but I was not willing to be another fad fitness and diet pusher. My own history with extreme fitness, body dysmorphia and bulimia were the reasons I had redirected my coaching methods. Whenever they would push me to launch a gimmicky fitness program, I couldn't help but feel haunted by my own bad choices a decade earlier.

Back in my mid-20's I was a hypocrite. Offering beneficial and effective personal training and nutrition strategies every day, all day, that I myself did not follow behind closed doors. The years of self-abuse through food and exercise coupled with the duplicity between my private and professional lives took a toll. Only when I hit rock bottom was I finally able to hear an inner voice of truth bubble up, subtle yet clear. At that moment, a Knowing, a deep spiritual knowing, arose. I Knew honesty and integrity were the only ways out of the mess I created.

Presently, though I felt frustrated, I didn't want to quit this new job. I saw this as a growth opportunity for us all, if only we could trust each other. They had the knowledge I needed about running an effective online company. I had captured a Knowing in my body through years of successful recovery and healing. Perhaps we could both get what we wanted.

As time passed, things fell into place. This strange (to me) technology allowed me to reach more people who could heal from the deleterious effects of diet dogmas and fitness fads. I loved teaching people how to experience more self-acceptance and grace. Watching them heal lit me up. I felt rooted in an inner Knowing that prompted me to honor my values, no matter the opposition.

Our success led the company to rebrand "me," create a new website and launch new programs. Together we'd reach more people and get more clicks. As amazing as this was, I still intuitively knew something was missing. So, I audaciously shared one of my dreams: I wanted to host live, in-person retreats. To my great surprise, this online company loved the idea.

My excitement was palpable and every cell in my body envisioned the event in detail. We'd gather in the beautiful mountains of Colorado with a small group of heart-centered women seeking rest, inquiry, growth, nature, and rejuvenation.

It was an exciting, creative time. The future was unfolding before me, and while I still had reservations about email funnels and social media, it all felt very bright and hopeful.

So, when they fired me and most of my team one day in September, it was an utter shock.

Suddenly, all the air was sucked out of me. The worst part was that they intended to abandon the clientele mid-program. Their reasons exposed what I had Known all along - they were way more into their clicks than into changing people's lives.

We had committed to a full year with our clients, and I intended to see it through. A week into flying solo, I realized that after all that time and exposure to the virtual world, I still had NO clue what I was doing on the 'backend' of things. I felt foolish, naive, and embarrassed to have been "let go," but letting everyone down was worse.

I had deep respect for how the team had edited, produced, and created everything that made online programming seamless and user-friendly. I believed, to keep my dreams alive, I needed to learn how to run an online business. The retreat was still possible, I told myself. All was not lost. It would just be postponed while I figured things out.

I hoped that an education in online business marketing would inspire me to create my own programs. Instead, I lost my zest completely.

I couldn't do it.

Actually, I could. Truth is, I didn't want to. I Knew it.

Once again, I was left questioning everything about my life.

Somehow my dream of an in-person retreat hitched itself to a successful online presence. I was professionally plagued by

FOMO. If I didn't have an online presence, was I relevant? Was I a failure if I quit after such a big investment?

I didn't want to be out of integrity. Force was no longer a tool I used to accomplish things, which meant everything about being online came to a screeching halt.

Fast forward to 2020. That year of seclusion wholeheartedly resurfaced my dream of hosting a retreat. My inner Knowing planted a seed: perhaps I could build a hybrid business model incorporating both in-person and online events.

My online prowess being rusty, I spent another year with another coach learning how to launch my programs online. A year chipping away at the requisite steps to prepare me for an in-person retreat. But I felt no closer than when I started. Again, I worried that I would fail.

It was during one of the final sessions for this entrepreneurial program when I finally blurted out that I wanted to host a retreat this year. My coach replied, "So, do it."

Initially, I was pissed. "'So do it?' Really?! What about the requisite steps? What about being professionally qualified to host such an event?!"

I didn't ask any of this. I just sat still, wondering why I often wait for permission from others to do what I Know I'm drawn to do. Why, with all my experiences of spiritual intuition, do I still desire external confirmation of internal Knowing?

Two things were true. I Knew I was supposed to host a retreat and I trusted my coach. Maybe I could do both. Trust her and myself. Yes, take the knowledge she's imparted, combine it with my experience and let the inner Knowing guide the process from here on!

Okay.

I Know how to proceed - this is how I healed from bulimia, extreme exercising, and self-abuse. Building a deeply trusting relationship with myself and with Divine Guidance allows me to feel the truth and let it land in my body.

I planned for the retreat, trusting Divine Guidance completely, asking for everything to fit into place - location, dates, pricing. I trusted that the right women, with ready hearts, would show up and sign up. As it came together, I knew that Spirit was dropping every detail into my heart, mind, and body.

In October 2022, I hosted the retreat of my dreams. The experience of watching the women receive all that they came for and more was miraculous. They reconnected with their body, mind, and soul. They played and rested in equal measure, experiencing the healing power of nature, community, and movement.

In 2014, I thought my life was falling apart. Now I see that a greater Knowing was under way, calling me to lean in and trust that subtle yet clear inner voice of truth. She is the one whispering the way toward the life I desire.

Missi Bantner
www.Livewholelifehealth.com
Missi@Livewholelifehealth.com

CHAPTER 12
FINDING MY WAY HOME

In May of 2021, I felt like I was suffocating. The world I had invested so much time and energy into was falling apart. My husband of sixteen years and I were filing for divorce after years of trying to come to terms with him being unfaithful. I was heartbroken, which triggered my unresolved 25 years of abuse from my first husband. The abusive words I had endured from my first marriage played on replay through my head "worthless, unlovable, unwanted." I felt God had forgotten me. Crying out to Him for guidance and comfort still left me feeling alone and angry. I was exhausted and felt like everything was pressing on me, and I couldn't get enough air. I had so many decisions to make, yet my brain was foggy. What was I going to do?

Two of my eight kids lived in Oregon, in the Portland area. I was panicked and wanted to run away from all the pain. Moving from Utah to Oregon would give me a fresh start and time to catch my breath. I retired from my job as a speech-language pathologist in the schools with an early retirement incentive. I would be husbandless, jobless, insurance-less, and homeless in a matter of weeks. As my house was listed for sale, I began looking for a rental in Oregon, only to discover that rentals were in high demand. Oregon has a first come, first serve law. Owners have to rent to the first qualified applicant. I had to locate a property, quickly fill out the application, and get it to the property manager. The catch is that every application comes with a fee of at least $50. When you are going through a divorce, every $50 counts. I started looking online for places, but I didn't know the area well enough to narrow the search, and I wasn't there to view the rentals in person. My adult kids were kind enough to look at a few for me.

But by the time I had arranged for them to view a property, the landlord would tell them that there were already several applications submitted.

I had to take a giant Leap of Faith to go somewhere brand new, with no job, downsizing from my comfortable big house to a tiny condo. Although I was angry at God, I didn't have anywhere else to turn to for help. I had to humble myself and look at evidence of Him directing my life in the past. I went to God. "God, I can't stay here. I need some air and space to breathe and figure out my next step in life. This house will be closing shortly. I am running out of time to find a place. Please help me to find a place. I check three websites multiple times a day to find a rental. Please put me where you know I need to be." Within a couple of days, a two-bedroom condo came up for rent. I felt compelled to fill out the application and submit it. Then I booked an appointment for my daughter to see it. She video-called me, so I could see the place and talk with the owner.

On Friday of that same week, the owner called me asking for my rental history and some proof of employment in Oregon.

"I don't have a rental history. I have owned a home for over 25 years and don't have a job in Oregon yet. But I am sure I can find one since there is a shortage of speech-language pathologists nationwide."

"Hmm, I'm not sure what to do. I have to do my due diligence. You are my preferred renter since the family living there previously was hard on the place. I would like a couple or a single person to rent it."

"I could send you the link to the house I am selling so you can see how I live. I will have the proceeds from the house, and I will get a job." I said, my heart rate escalating and my mind racing for some solution. But I couldn't think of anything else I could do or say at that moment.

"Let's not worry about this over the weekend. Let me think about it, and I will call you back on Monday." He reassured me.

As soon as I hung up the phone, I started praying; I mean really praying out loud. I poured it all out to God. I kept explaining the situation to God as if He didn't already know. "I can't give the owner any documents he requests since they don't exist. If this condo is where you want me to be, you will have to make it happen. I feel like this would be a good place for me, and it's close to my kids." I petitioned, "there is nothing else I can do." I resolved to trust God and not fret over the weekend. I continued to pray that prayer in my heart all weekend.

On Monday, my phone rang. It was the condo owner, "Janet, I don't know why but I will just go with it and rent you the condo. I will email you the contract, and we can discuss the details."

"Thank you, I promise you will not be sorry," I said as I held back tears. The owner had no idea what a relief that was to me. He may not have known why he felt he should "just go with it." But I knew why; God had touched his heart and convinced him to do something that seemed to go against his typical rational way of thinking but was the right thing. He took a Leap of Faith.

I moved to that small condo in Oregon and lived by myself for the first time. I reflected on all the times I had wished for a little me time to myself through the years of raising eight kids. I had so much of it that I hardly knew what to do with myself. At first, I was in so much pain that I didn't appreciate that little condo. As the days passed, I realized it was the perfect spot to heal.

I got a job in the schools and spent the rest of my time walking in the woods and nature of Oregon. Every morning outside my bedroom window, I heard birds singing and the chattering of squirrels from the wooded green space out back. I realized how grateful I was for that sweet alarm clock each day. I built a closer relationship with God and saw His hand daily in tender mercies. I slept a lot. It felt as if I had been sleep-deprived for years. Stress will do that to a body. I worked on healing my trauma and betrayal. I made amazing new friends, started to laugh, and felt loved and lovable again. By the end of the school year, June 2022, I felt like a new person. I decided my time in the beautiful Pacific Northwest was complete and moved back to a new area of Utah, closer to more of my kids and grandkids. God helped me find my home in Utah through unusual circumstances again.

My older daughters summed up the experience when they said, "Mom when you left Utah, we were so worried about you. You were a hot mess, but now you are a happy whole new better you!"

I learned that trusting God is always the right move. How many times in scripture are we told, "trust in the Lord"? We know He is everlasting and does not change. I was blessed that He not only found me a home, but I found my way home back to Him. If we have enough faith that the Lord has our best interest in mind, we can trust Him. Do you trust God even when the next step is difficult, and you don't have all the answers?

Janet Pippin
www.desirable-life.com
janet@desirable-life.com

CHAPTER 13

THE POWER OF PERCEPTION

Questioning everything is not new to me. I am a curious person who anticipates a new day. I had just moved into a new place and obtained my business license on January 23, 2020, to practice Massage Therapy. Now, I was able to attract new clients and rebuild my business. Manifest 2020 was my motto. Then on March 4 the beginning of the end happened. I did not know it that day – but the Wuhan Virus – later COVID-19 - hit our province. The fear of infections rose and on March 28, 2020, the government shut down all businesses and "locked us down" in our homes.

I was in an emotional state of panic that I could not define. Not because of the virus – but because of the unknown. Would I have enough money? How will I handle being isolated? How can I possibly survive? Like a tornado, all that was familiar was being tossed into a whirlwind of essential or not essential. Institutions of learning, worship, and congregating are all considered non-essential! My work closed – non-essential.

Living alone, in a new place, I was left to my own thoughts. Everything familiar to me was uprooted and thrown into question. Even people I thought were grounded and stable began speaking in ways that were frightful and without hope. Their fear and anger added to the winds of my storm.

By the third week into lockdown – I crashed. I lay on the sofa not wanting to move. I was not depressed. I was simply immobile. Overtaken with the weight of the unknown. I stayed there for five days. Watching endless hours of television. I questioned why I was there. I asked myself over and again what was stopping me from "catching" up on all the work I could be doing. You know –

those mundane tasks like sorting through stuff, cleaning out closets, writing a book. Taking advantage of all the "time" I had on my hands. No. I laid on that couch like I was glued to the fabric. At 10:00 pm on the fifth day, I rose up and said out loud: "Enough. I am done with that."

I then cleaned my kitchen, swept the floor, tidied the house, and went to bed. I slept like a rock.

It was one of my turning points in 2020.

At that moment, it was as though God lifted me up and said walk. In that rising, I chose life. Yet, I questioned everything. Everywhere I looked, I felt my internal self—angry, sad, fearful, longing, and most devasting of all, hopeless. I felt alone, unsupported, and unfulfilled. I felt abandoned by my faith, my hope, and by God. What's it all about??

The next turning point.

With nothing else to do, I went outside and planted a garden. My hands tilled the soil. As it coursed through my fingers the dry grunge of earth penetrated my nostrils with the promise of change. After days of preparation, it was time to plant seeds. I created rows, carefully placed the seeds in position, and gently covered them with soil. I thanked them for the job they were about to do – the job of sprouting. I looked over the work I had done and felt so good. I was proud of what I had accomplished even before the evidence of the garden had shown itself.

Note to self. When I focus on one thing at a time, do the work, and enjoy the process, I am encouraged.

Then, I surrendered my garden to God. I believed He would water it with rain, and provide sunshine, warmth, and just the right amount of wind to make the plants strong. I had no control over those forces bigger than myself. Those seeds became sprouts and then they became plants. I became grateful. I visited my garden every morning and basked in its progress.

In good time, the plants sprouted and then flowers began showing up on many of the plants. This meant bees were on their way! I was in for another lesson – the dance of the bees.

The bees came. The garden was abuzz with activity. Honey

bees circled the flowers like a dance partner looking for a mate. Then, they would dive in–literally—to the base of the flower. They kissed the stamens over and over again with a ferocity I had never before taken the time to witness. With complete abandon, I sat down in the grass and watched my plants come alive with activity that delighted me beyond words.

I had to laugh at how some of the bees' bellies were so full and yet they would not leave the flowers. It seemed they would fall to the ground at times rather than make it back to the hive. Other times, they would dive into the flower and then back away and seem to dance with incredible joy at their find before diving back into the heart of the flower. They buzzed loudly with joy, and it was infectious!

My garden flourished. I thanked God for the sun, the warmth, and the rain. My sunflowers grew to be at least eight feet tall! I had never seen such large sunflowers. I stood with them facing the sun, basking in gratitude and appreciation while absorbing the warmth and the light.

One brilliant summer morning, I recognized how much I had grown. The world pandemic that swarmed my world made me open my eyes to see in new ways they had not seen before. My ears began to hear sounds they had missed. The GREAT PAUSE I call this time. A time to Stop and to Notice – what am I hearing, what am I seeing? Then from that new space of appreciation, growth, and faith, move forward into the next moment.

I learned that though I am solo, I am not alone for a single second. I stand on the ground of generations of wisdom gone before me. Those that fertilized our growth paused to let us know what they knew. God is at my side creating miracles every moment of every day. When I choose to look for them, I see them. They are everywhere and living is miraculous. The great PAUSE 2020 – rather than a time of production became my time of great introspection. I learned so much from my garden.

2020. A full sentence in four numbers. Numbers that are used to explain vision or reflection as in: "he has 20/20 vision," or the well-known saying: "Hindsight is 20/20." A year that began with anticipation and belief in what I could manifest. It ended with humility and gratitude. In the large scheme of things, I am a dim light that could easily be overlooked but if I do not shine, I contribute to the darkness.

I stand on the fertile soil of our ancestors, their experiences, wisdom, and faith. I was given a chance to pivot my business and chose to become a Grief Recovery Specialist, an online counselor for those who have suffered significant loss. That year was a test of my faith, of my belief.

Do you know that the Bible says "Be not afraid" 365 times? That is once for each day. Those five days spent lying on the couch, afraid, was my walk in the valley of darkness. When I stood up and decided "No More," I walked in faith. I took action to move forward. No matter how the winds blow or what it is that may swarm us, I am not alone. Isolation taught me that the ripple effect one has on the other is profound. People need people. The unknown is not the worst thing. Far worse is not having hope.

Being fully present in this moment and taking in the glory of God in what is around me is the brilliant sunshine of each day. It is the greatest gift I can give to myself and those around me. The honey bees taught me how magnificent it is to be abuzz with passion for the abundance we have in front of us. The great pause of 2020. The time that allowed me to face my turmoils, ask for help and stand tall in the face of any storm. I look at it in awe and wonder.

2020 nourished me anew. I had been labelling my worth by the perception of my life's circumstances and experiences. But this garden showed me that I am not defined by anything other than the depths of the Father's love for me.

The harvest is inevitable. I will reap what I have sown. Until that day, I am here, to bask in the glory of this moment. Standing as tall as the sunflower and abuzz with anticipation. It is all about perception.

Thank you, COVID-19, for putting the pause in 2020 and to you God for being the nail in my pivot.

Janine Brisebois
https://www.thatgriefrecoverylady.com
thatgriefrecoverylady@gmail.com

CHAPTER 14
FALLING UP - STEPPING INTO THE SCARY, LOOKING STUPID, AND CREATING SPACE FOR SUCCESS

I kissed my four little kids goodbye on a cold February morning as I hopped onto a long-distance bus. This was the first time I would be away from my little ones for a long time. It was 2018, and for eight years I had invested my time and body into either nursing or being pregnant. Getting away was a rare occurrence. As I stepped onto the bus, my hands felt curiously empty. For years, a baby or toddler had occupied the area where my quiet, little purse nestled.

"I feel like I'm missing something?" I thought to myself as I settled into my seat.

I scrolled through the list in my mind once more, all the while shifting awkwardly in my seat. I could not get rid of this pervasive gut feeling that had plagued me since I made the decision to leave home for a few days and attend a Christian Startup Conference in Heidelberg, Germany.

"Why am I even doing this? I know nothing about business... I'm just a simple homeschooling mom with four kids." The thoughts felt like they were tightening around the synapses in my brain, enveloping them, consuming them.

"NO!" With that word, I pushed aside the unease I was feeling, "I can do this... even homeschooling moms can pitch businesses!"

I started to replace the worried thoughts with developing confidence.

"So, what if I fail? Failure doesn't exist in this."

The bus ride went by faster than expected, and I arrived at the station to meet my sister Taylor, my partner in doing new and sometimes silly things. We checked into our lodging for the weekend and headed out immediately to the conference venue: a big commercial-looking building that was part church, part office building, nestled between a freeway and a field.

With butterflies in my stomach, we walked up the stairs to be greeted by dozens of youthful faces, registered ourselves, grabbed our lanyards, and made our way into the conference space.

I don't know many people who feel right at home in big crowds of strangers. I certainly feel out of my league every time. I felt squeezed, like someone was pushing me out of the comfort of my own skin. IIn my mind's eye, I saw the tempting vision of me walking out and never coming back. No one would notice.

Except that my experience had anchored this truth in my soul: Exactly in those moments when everything in me is screaming, "Give up! Flee! Run away!" I know I need to dive in – because that is where the next big shift is going to happen.

I scanned the clusters of people scattered throughout the foyer and event hall, and a stone fell into my gut. "Gosh, I don't belong here."

All I could see were young, bright-eyed MBA students from the local university and middle-aged "business" men in their button-up shirts and jeans. There were maybe one or two women closer to my age, but we were clearly a minority.

Not for the first time that day, I pushed away the constricting thoughts and instead remembered a story my mom told me about her Czech father, my Grandpa Joe.

This big, gruff Eastern European also happened to be a serial entrepreneur. One day, when I was still a child, he showed up on the doorstep of our 100-year-old red farmhouse - unannounced, recently divorced, and apparently lonely. He was not the type for random visits.

And he didn't waste time getting to the reason for his visit. "How can I make friends?" he blurted out to my mom in his thick Czech accent. After his divorce, he suddenly found himself lonely and unable to socialize.

My mom, always the clever and quick-witted woman, responded, "People like to talk about themselves. Just ask them questions about themselves – that's the quickest way to make friends."

I took a deep breath. If my socially awkward Czech Grandpa could do it in his old age, so could I in my 30s. I resolved to be a learner and ask questions. You're never out of place if you position yourself as the learner.

With this mindset, I found my first victim. The man stood apart from the other groups, his only company a green palm tree, meant to warm up the commercial feeling of the room. Immediately, I grabbed a cup of coffee and meandered towards him.

"Hey! I'm Dani, what's your name?"

"Nice to meet you, Dani, I'm Bruce."

"What are you doing here, Bruce?"

"My wife and I have been serving for years as missionaries in a city in Cambodia. We noticed that no matter how many Bibles we hand out and church programs we run, the women and children still suffer economically. In order to afford a decent education, the moms often have to resort to the sex industry to make ends meet. We wanted to do something about that. So, we took the approach of starting a T-shirt factory in order to help change their economic situation. With this business, we offer them the chance to get out of the sex trade. We train them, and we even offer childcare and many other benefits. Recently, we connected this business with the German market, and it has just exploded in growth. Today we're the number one employer of that city. So that's why I'm here, to share what is possible with business and what God wants to do with it to impact the nations."

With that simple story, my heart felt like it was about to leap out of my chest.

All the thoughts in me were shouting, "THIS IS IT!!"

Those few minutes shifted my trajectory. With just this one story. That one encounter. I felt all my insecurities melt away.

"This is where I belong!" Among the pioneers and business creators called to create wealth and prosperity. For hope and future.

I realized it didn't matter whether I was a homeschooling mom, a young MBA student, or a middle-aged man.

What mattered was that I said no to fear and chose courage.

I briefly imagined the women and children in abject poverty in Cambodia. Had my new acquaintance not had the courage to start something new, something never done before, where would they be today? Still selling their bodies - and their dignity - to Western tourists just to put food on the table?

But someone's courage gave them hope and a future.

And that's what I would do. I've chosen courage again and again, sometimes with shaking knees - because I know this is where God wants to use you and me to make a difference.

From that moment on, I was on a mission to keep pushing into the scary.

Less than 24 hours after that conversation, I stood in a public bathroom stall, legs akimbo, arms stretched in the shape of a V to the heavens. I took a minute to breathe slowly and prepare my mind. As I left the stall, I chuckled to myself, thinking "If anyone saw me power posing over the toilet, that would be hilarious!"

My turn had come to pitch my business idea to a small group of investors - in my second language, German, in front of an audience of about 100 people!

Praying that I would sound articulate and make sense to the crowd, I presented my horrible business idea. I say horrible, because just a week before I didn't even know what a pitch was. I scrambled to formulate a business idea that I could present to a panel of investors who had 40+ years of business experience.

With colorful slides and a funny accent, I pitched a vague and, frankly, somewhat confusing business idea that had no real strategy of producing revenue.

"Uhh, thank you, Frau Goeppert." was the panel's polite comment on my pitch.

Beaming with confidence and exhilaration, I returned to my

seat to watch the other pitches.

"I freakin did it!" I thought to myself.

In comparison, my pitch wasn't the worst, but it certainly didn't even come close to most of the others. Not surprisingly, I didn't win the pitch competition. But inside I felt like I had just conquered the world!

What other mom goes out and pitches a business in front of a crowd??

Despite the fact that I wholly embraced and loved my role as mama (and still do), with that one terrifying act of pitching a terrible business idea I added to my mama identity. No longer was I just an appendage to my children or my husband. I was an entrepreneur!

Because of that event, the stories that were shared, and the opportunity it gave me to believe in something a little bigger, do something a little scarier, my trajectory shifted. I started to build out my own successful virtual event company, Risen Events, and I'm loving it.

What's your scary, your obstacle? Because your story, your challenge, your fear may be the exact thing needed for someone's breakthrough.

"So be strong and courageous! Do not be afraid and do not panic before them. For the LORD your God will personally go ahead of you. He will neither fail you nor abandon you." --
Deuteronomy 31:6

Dani Goeppert
Risenevents.com
Dani@risenevents.com

CHAPTER 15
UNDER GOD'S DIRECTION

"Sometimes it's the people no one can imagine anything of who do the things that no one can imagine" - Enigma.

You might say my Leap of Faith was the result of a direct call. More like God saying, "Hey, Ray! I'm HERE!" Certain experiences can change the course of your life, and that's what happened to me at 4:30 PM on November 19, 2010.

That afternoon, I awaited a call about purchasing a piece of land in Arkansas as an investment. I was unsure about my decision and wished I could discuss it with my wife. Unfortunately, that wasn't possible because she'd been called back to Costa Rica, her native country, to care for her sick mother.

About a week before, I had asked God for a sign whether to buy the property or not. I hadn't received anything I could interpret as a sign one way or another, and I was getting nervous. God didn't seem to show up. I decided I was on my own, and I didn't feel very confident about that.

The call was scheduled for 5:30 PM.

At 4:30, I sat at my desk, still wondering what to do. Suddenly, I saw the words "BELIEVE IN ME" appear directly in front of my eyes. The phrase was clear and unmistakable. It lasted only a moment, and then it vanished.

My first thought was to ask myself, what did I see? Did I really see it? "BELIEVE IN ME!"

Just thinking about it gave me goosebumps—a quick breeze-like feeling across the hair on my arms.

Did I really see those words?

I leaned back in my chair for what seemed like an hour, going over and over what had just happened.

Okay, I saw it!

Was it real?

Yes!

I'd asked God for a sign, and He'd answered my prayer in a way I couldn't have predicted. The experience made me see myself and my relationship with God differently. The Ray Comeau I knew—the man my wife, my family, and my friends knew—could never be the same.

Of course, my wife was the first person I called. She accepted what I told her, maybe not with the same level of belief I had, but then again, how could she understand? I sensed the same skepticism when I shared my story with friends.

A few weeks later, I made an appointment with Father Charles at our church. I went in not knowing exactly how to explain my experience. When I told him, what he said surprised me.

"So, Ray, you think you're the only one?" He pointed to a bookcase filled with over a hundred books written by people who'd had encounters with God.

Our conversation lasted only about fifteen minutes, and I left feeling let down and sorry for him. Why was he not as excited as I was? If he had been an evangelist, he would have showcased me to his followers.

I thanked God for letting me know of His presence around me. I not only had a mental belief that God existed, but also the certainty that I had experienced Him in a physical way.

Despite my encounter with God, my next six years were so filled with the busyness of life, I didn't really have much time to make drastic changes. Still, I never forgot how God had shown Himself to me.

In January of 2016, I decided to retire and move to Costa Rica. Before I left, I stopped to say goodbye to a customer/friend I'd known for over eight years. Our conversation was never short on words or topics.

Pete began by telling me his son was reading the Quran. This led me to relate the story of my call from God six years earlier.

He came back to me to ask what I had done about it. "What do you mean, Pete?"

"Ray, you were given a gift! You need to do something with it!"

I'd repeated the story over a hundred times and had never received such a response. I felt as if I had just awakened from sleep or been given a slap on my cheek.

"Oh my God, Pete! You're RIGHT!"

We made our farewells, and I drove home not knowing what to think of this wake-up call.

I tossed and turned all night. The next day, I awoke with the idea of writing a book.

As I wrote over the next few months, I kept thinking, 'Why me?'

You see, I'm an unlikely candidate for God to choose to write a book. In high school, I needed to study harder than my friends. I used to pray for some kind of transformation. I didn't know why school was difficult for me until I discovered at age fifty that I've had ADHD—attention deficit/hyperactivity disorder—all my life.

God may indeed have a sense of humor. As the saying goes, God doesn't call the qualified; He qualifies those He calls.

My "retirement" has brought the transformation I used to pray for. Now I'm a writer, a speaker, and am actively involved with prison ministry and helping ex-offenders.

My first book, *What Bad We Do*, will be released in 2023. It addresses many of the problems that cause such heartache to men, women, and children in our society today. My second and third books are already in progress.

As I move forward to answer God's call on my life, He continues to open doors and connect me with amazing people.

One such connection came through LinkedIn back in March 2019. I connected with Pastor Willie Simpson, National Director of Outreach Reentry Ministry, which has helped ex-offenders since 1988. The first week we emailed. The next week we started to talk by phone and have spoken almost daily since. He invited me to be a keynote speaker at his 2019 National Executive Committee Conference in Muscle Shoals, Alabama.

While there, I was voted to be Education Coordinator, and best of all, I met a wonderful group of people who have become long-distance friends I talk with weekly. One year later, I became National Administrator of Outreach Reentry Ministry. I now serve as National Education Coordinator. Pastor Willie Simpson and I will always remain friends in God.

As you can see, a Leap of Faith can lead you on a journey to help others looking for answers.

Take your Leap of Faith! GRAB IT! Don't let go!

Ray Comeau
www.oursoulsdirection.com
raycomeauwriting@gmail.com

CHAPTER 16
A HEART OF STONE FOR A HEART OF FLESH

"We all, with unveiled faces, are looking as in a mirror at the glory of the Lord and are being transformed into the same image from glory to glory; this is from the Lord who is the Spirit." -- 2 Corinthians 3:18 (Christian Standard Bible)

From the outside, I looked great.

I was always moving forward. I was active in church, a leader in Sunday school, a choir director, and even volunteered in church administration.

I'd graduated college, paid for it all myself working four jobs at the same time, and after graduation was now continuing to work full time. My life was one where I consistently planned, achieved goals, prayed, and set out to have a life with family and friends.

While I seemed fine, my heart was buried in darkness.

I didn't have meaningful conversations with people as my heart desired: I worked jobs where I listened and never spoke and I didn't even try having conversations with others, I couldn't be present.

The family trips and relationships seemed real, yet I didn't know how much vulnerability, love, responsibility, and connection I was missing.

No one knew how many men's hearts I had broken, or the lack of connection with my friends.

On the outside I was fine, inside I was numb.

Even though I grew up with a caring mom and a hard-working dad, I didn't grow up in a loving home. I was constantly in fear. Fear that I wouldn't do the right thing. Fear that I wouldn't sit the right way. Fear that my brother or sister would cry, and I'd be blamed for it. Fear that if I cried or asked for anything, that would be, "the end of it."

I was always afraid, and in fear of unfair punishment. I became hyper-vigilant, always on guard and always guarded. My worldview was formed, and I learned I couldn't trust men's words, actions, nor character, and women were distant and unavailable.

I was alone, the world was dark, and there was nothing I could do about it.

I always felt like I was walking through life in a dark tunnel. If I looked far enough, I could see that there was a glimpse of light, but I truly felt that there was so much evil in this world, that God was just so distant, and so was the light.

As a result, I walked around protecting myself.

I didn't let anyone into my heart, and I kept everyone at arm's length. I could sit with a friend face to face and just share things about my family or other people, but never anything about what I was dealing with. I would simply listen all day long.

I could listen but I could never speak. I could never share my heart.

I assumed all relationships would go the way of my home life, so when it came to romantic relationships I was never trusting, and I broke their hearts before they broke mine.

I was isolated and numb. On the outside, I was smiling, but I just couldn't feel. I took everything as entertainment, a distraction. Everything was outside of me. If there was anything to smile about or to be sad about it: was outside of me. My heart couldn't feel anything.

This was my life and it continued until I met my now husband: as we grew closer, I saw for the first time a glimpse of the love that I knew God had promised in the Bible. Within the first months, we both knew God was orchestrating beautiful love between us and was I excited!

This is everything I wanted right?

He said he was committed, and I trusted him. His gorgeous eyes saw all of me, and instead of rejecting me, he stayed! My heart was completely open.

Could my life really shift just by falling in love? I hoped so… and as much as I wanted this to be true… the old thoughts and feelings that I'd grown up with started to speak and doubts started to creep in.

"Can I trust this," they said.

"Can you really stay open," they asked.

They even found a voice in a family member who said to me, "Is this really the right guy for you? You've only known him for a short time. You don't really know all of him."

The seeds of doubt began to grow like a fast-spreading weed. I've since learned that what we hold onto grows. If it's an empowering thing, it'll grow. When we hold onto what is not good: the doubts, the lies, the negative thinking, they also grow.

These weeds of doubt joined the decades of striving and cold-heartedness compelled me to once again break another heart.

We were moving toward marriage, and I believed, once more, that there was no hope, that I'd have to settle, and I began to see my past happening all over again. I was disheartened thinking things could never be as I dreamed.

I acted on my doubts and broke his heart before he could break mine.

I sabotaged the relationship; the marriage was called off, and I thought this was another ending.

Life, however, is full of grace and love. I knew it was time to run.

I was faced with a decision: I could run away, or I could run into the arms of the one who had my heart. I could run and hide, just as I had time and time again. Continuing the cycle of pain and hurt.

Or I could run to love.

Run to someone who loved me, along with a community he had built for us on a foundation of unconditional love and acceptance.

Or… I could choose to show up in my guilt, shame and brokenness.

The biggest leap I took was to trust that life could be a life of

83

love and acceptance.

I decided to take that leap. I said Yes. That one, single Yes opened the door…

To community.

To myself.

To healing.

…and ultimately to God.

I began a journey of healing and a leap to a new life.

I went to Celebrate Recovery, a one-year Christian 12-Step Program.

I flew to Tennessee for a seven-day personal growth intensive at a place called Onsite.

I moved across the country, in order to be in the same city as my fiancé and go to counseling.

I led God in.

While at Onsite, I was reading a book called *Captivating*, and in it they quoted Hosea 2:16, which says, *"In that day," declares the LORD, "you will call me 'my husband' you will no longer call me 'my master.' (New Living Translation)*

Later that day I sat on a wooden swing made for two. I was thinking about everything that happened that led me to being here. I began to see my favorite things, the swing beneath me, the rustling of the leaves, the wind in my hair and I became present to the moment and all it had to offer.

I could hear God's soft whisper, and He asked me if I would open my heart to Him if I would allow Him in and accept Him to be my husband, and for me to be his bride.

I knew that I had previously chosen God as my Savior and I had given him my life…Now I give Him my heart.

I had reached a level of intimacy with my fiancé, and I could hear God whisper an invitation, "I want this intimacy with you."

God is the creator of love, right?

As much as God cared about my romantic life, he cared more about me getting to know His love from Him. He desired that I get to know Him and His heart towards me.

I no longer dream of the beautiful things that could be…I now experience them. I get to embrace the moments, the emotions, and the relationships in my life.

Betsy Souder
worldclassspeakacademy.com
betsy@worldclassspeakeracademy.com

CHAPTER 17
(NOT) PLAYING IT TOO SAFE

My husband Steve and I had lived in Southern California for most of our lives when we decided to move to Oregon. We both felt the tug that we would move out of California years before it happened. Moving to a new state is challenging for anyone, and our complications included being a blended family. Still, I felt the pull to find a new home, a fresh start.

My first choice was Tennessee. I loved the idea because we both liked being outdoors and enjoyed the warmer weather. But when Steve's two children moved to Oregon, visiting them changed the plan entirely. Oregon was where we could be closer to them. My dream of living in Tennessee would not become a reality, and I hoped God had a better plan.

This was the first move for Steve and me, which was extensive and out of state. We left behind our support systems, friends, family, church family, beaches, weather (no snow!), and our way of life.

While we knew we were taking a HUGE leap of faith, we also believed in our hearts that if we were in God's will, He would provide and open up the doors before us. Saying and believing this was easy until we encountered opposition. We found ourselves asking each other, "Are we doing the right thing? Is this the right time?" wanting to reassure each other. We simultaneously walked out being in God's will while having things go wrong or not the way we had planned or prayed.

Over the subsequent two months, we listed our house for sale three different times. Two buyers backed out after beginning the process, leaving us in limbo. When we listed our home for the third time, it sold in just a couple of weeks. However, we were a little gun-shy to finalize plans in Oregon before the move in case the third buyer backed out. Steve and I had to make many tentative decisions until we moved further along in the escrow timeline, tiptoeing through the process. We were praying and asking God what to do each step of the way and to provide what we would need in Oregon once we moved. He was Faithful and would give us direction for the next step and the next.

We closed escrow on our home at the end of August and arrived in Oregon two days later. We rented a house for eight months from a wonderful family. We shared the same Christian beliefs and were thankful he chose to rent to us in such a tight rental market. God led us to this family, and we were so grateful to have a home to live in until we could find a home to purchase, which we did within a year. God was faithful again!

In spite of all of our good fortune, if I had known how hard the move was going to be emotionally and physically, I don't think I would have moved at the time. I knew there would be challenges in Oregon but starting over in a new area with a different culture, different church, and making new friends, had turned out to be much harder on my heart than I imagined. I was grieving the loss of what we left behind and praying that God would heal my heart and show us how to thrive in our new adventure. It took me about two and a half years to feel like I belonged.

Finding the right long-term job that fit me like a glove was much more challenging than it had ever been. This was strange and unnerving territory; it felt like I was doing something wrong or missing something. When we lived in California, I would hold a job for 5-10 years before moving on. Sometimes as a business closed or a better position came along, I would apply for the job and be hired. But Oregon was a completely different ball game.

On one particular occasion, I was at a Women's Retreat with my church, and while praying, I heard God say to me, "You're playing it too safe."

Whoa! I questioned God, how was I playing it too safe? I reminded Him of my courage to move out of California, what we left behind, and how much harder it was than I anticipated. I asked Him what He meant, as I was confused and uncertain. I didn't understand exactly what this meant at the time, but I did get a better understanding about a year later.

In the fall of 2019, I knew I would be leaving my current job soon. The leadership in the company I was working for left a lot to be desired, and I dreaded being in that office. The wind was quickly going out of my sails, and soon I felt the need to resign. I felt obligated to stay for various reasons, including paying my bills. I didn't have another job lined up, and at this point, I made a vow that I would never work for anyone again as an employee. Because of my background in accounting and bookkeeping, I believed I could start my own bookkeeping business, run it the way that worked for me, have it align with my values, and set my schedule and earnings. But not this soon, and not this abruptly. I had planned on taking my time, relying on my income from a regular job, to get everything set up before I took the leap.

One day as I was sitting at my desk at work, I was speaking to God, and I told Him how I felt trapped with no other choices. I believe I heard Him say, "You have a choice."

I quickly asked Him, "What? Do I have a choice? Really? What does that look like? Can I resign?" Yes, all these questions were going through my head in rapid fire succession! At that moment, I felt God was telling me, "You choose."

This was a HUGE turning point for me going forward. I resigned two days later and never looked back. I started Totally Booked bookkeeping, and my only regret is that I hadn't done it sooner. God sent me my first client within a month of starting my business. This was when I recalled what God was speaking to me a year earlier about "Playing it too safe." Often for me to take a risk, I would have to do all the research, pray, ask friends, etc., before making a move. Don't misunderstand, there is wisdom in Godly counsel, and I highly recommend praying. But how often do we need everything to line up in our perspective when God tells us to take that Leap of Faith, and aren't His fatherly arms plenty big to catch us? Even if we fail, God doesn't punish His kids for trying! He will get us back on track.

In 2021, my husband Steve and I moved from Oregon to Arkansas. After all that work and time, Oregon just wasn't the place for us.

Ya'll, I never imagined us in the South, and I needed to know someone in the area for me to have a point of connection once we moved. I was nudged by Holy Spirit one morning at church to visit our friends from California who had moved to Arkansas to see if we could see ourselves living there. Once we returned from our trip, we sold our home and moved two months later. We learned many lessons from the first interstate move we implemented when moving across the country! When we got here, we didn't have a house to move into, but God provided a short-term stay with a friend's family. Within a few months, He provided a home for us to purchase in a crazy real estate market. I believe God honored our trust in Him in so many ways!

At the end of 2022, I began to sense God was shifting me and my business. He is leading me to offer business consulting to help entrepreneurs and small business owners to advance God's Kingdom in the Marketplace. I don't have all the details of what this looks like yet. However, I have a proven track record that where He leads, He equips and provides.

I have been on the best adventure with God since I have chosen not to play small and start taking some risks. I heard Him speak to me recently: "Get comfortable with being uncomfortable." I had feared many things, and fear kept me from my destiny. Often, we have a choice but do not move forward out of fear.

How we show up matters, and the fact that we show up speaks volumes to those around us. We always have more options than we think. And sometimes it's better to leap than stand and think.

My encouragement to you is, don't play it too safe! Leap into His faithfulness!

Cheryl Ziegler
totallybookedpnw.com
cheryl@cherylziegler.com

CHAPTER 18
JUST LEAP! GOD IS IN THE GAP!

You may wonder if you can count on God to catch you when you fall. I have found that He is with me whenever I take a leap. God is with me, and He makes up the difference when me when I fall short. God will show up in the gap. There have been many leaps of faith in my life. Large and small leaps have moved my life forward. Every time I needed to make a change or do something different, it took a measure of faith to make the move. Every time I have faced a challenge, God has shown up in the GAP! The Oxford dictionary defines a gap as "space or breaks in continuity." It is the divergence or disparity between where we are, and where God wants to take us. The gap is where God is found. It is when we have exhausted our answers and we have no more strength. We must rest on the promises of God when we are in the gap.

Sometimes people step out to do wonderful and miraculous things with no money, no formal education, and no help. They leap with nothing but sheer faith and drive to accomplish their big dreams and goals. Sometimes they must do it afraid! They leap hoping that the net would appear in the gap. I have had my own gap experiences with God. I am sure you have had some gap experiences too!

Let's talk about the times that I found God in the gap. My college experience was quite a leap! I was the first person in my family to attend college. It was exciting to be living away from home, but it was also a little scary. I was away at school, living on campus, and making my own decisions. I was always a good student, and going away to college was my dream, but that first year was difficult. The studies were rigorous, and I had difficulty managing my time. I failed a class for the first time in my life and faced academic probation. My scholarship and educational goals were in jeopardy. It was a very discouraging time, causing me to doubt if I even belonged in college. I spent the summer after freshman year making up those classes. I graduated from college and eventually returned for a graduate degree. God was with me, and I persevered.

Marriage was a leap for me! I grew up in a single-parent home, and the marriages around me left something to be desired. God gave me the faith to take the marriage leap. There were so many times that God had to meet us in the gap—with mercy and grace. There are many challenges that God brought us through – difficult pregnancies, post-partum depression, financial challenges, health challenges, wayward children—and some problems I can't even recall. God was in the gap every time.

The mention of cancer stops me in my tracks. The men in my life—my father, my grandfather, and most recently my husband battled cancer. Those questions appeared once again – Why? God carried us through those years of treatment. God was in the gap.

Writing and publishing a book was my most recent leap from the ledge of comfort and safety. Journaling is my favorite pastime, and I always thought "one day I'll write a book." After the death of my husband in August 2020, my grief counselor suggested that I write about my feelings. I began to journal about my experiences of grief and loss— anger, sadness, loneliness, etc., This brought some relief, and I felt that maybe I should write a book and share my thoughts with others.

I felt like Peter when Jesus was calling him to step out of the boat. Writing the book was my "out of the boat" experience. I prayed "God, I can only do it if you help me." This was not the time, and it certainly was not the book I thought I would be writing. I was dealing with my grief, and hoping to get back to living when this book began to find its way out of my mind and onto the blank pages of my journal. My book "Walk into Your New" was truly a leap of faith. It has been a profound and life-changing experience. It was a personal leap, an emotional leap, and a financial leap. God is still with me.

The book was birthed from the pain of losing my husband to cancer. We were married for thirty-three years—so many memories! The leap was to write from my heart, exposing my grief experiences. It was cathartic and it allowed the wounds to air out. My emotions were raging! There was pain, anger, loneliness, and disappointment for all to see. There are so many books about grief– each person telling their individual stories. The books all asking the same questions – Why did my person have to die? Why now? What if? What now? Even in the questions, God brought comfort. He is in the gap and he hovers somewhere between what I can do, and what He wants to achieve.

I stepped out and joined Joy Morgan's "Write That Book Challenge." The challenge walked a group of us through writing a book in 3 months. It was quite a journey! Sometimes the writing assignments were completed and at other times, I was ready to quit. As I began to make progress with the writing challenge, my computer died. It was the morning I was leaving for the writing retreat. The big blue screen of death appeared, and my manuscript disappeared. When that happened, my first thought was "maybe this just isn't supposed to be." I was going to the writing retreat with nothing written on the page. It was so embarrassing! I was six weeks in, and I had to start all over! Fear tried to overtake me, and the "imposter syndrome" began to take over and sabotage my process. I wondered, "who wants to hear from me?" I was feeling defeated! Why was this happening? Why is the enemy fighting me on this?

At this point, I remembered that God was my partner in this book project. My part was to finish the book. God brought me this far and he would not fail me now! I persevered and continued my assignment. My story was not just for me, it was for those who would read my book and find the strength to live on after their loss. If this book was going to be published, God would need to be my partner.

In the gap, God provides grace, access, and power! There is grace for every situation. His lovingkindness will protect us against any danger and helps us to bear the pain. We are complete and fulfilled in him and we can find our rest in his grace.

"My grace is sufficient for thee: for my strength is made perfect in weakness" --2 Corinthians 12:9

"Thou, therefore, my son, be strong in the grace that is in Christ Jesus" --2 Timothy 2:1

In the gap, there is access to God. Favor is not fair, but it comes just in time. God cares about what concerns us and He gives us the grace we need.

"Let us, therefore, draw near with boldness unto the throne of grace that we may receive mercy, and may find grace to help us in time of need." –Hebrews 4:16

"Blessed is the man who thou choosest and causest to approach unto thee, That he may dwell in thy courts: We shall be satisfied with the goodness of thy house, Thy holy temple" -- Psalm 65:4

"One thing have I asked of Jehovah, that will I seek after That I may dwell in the house of Jehovah all the days of my life, To behold the beauty of Jehovah, And to inquire in his temple" -- Psalm 27:4

In the gap, there is the power of the covenant that God gives His children. Always remember with profound respect that God is our source. He gives us the power to get wealth, to enjoy the provisions and our appointed lot.

"But thou shalt remember Jehovah thy God, for it is he that giveth thee power to get wealth; that he may establish his covenant which he sware unto thy fathers, as at this day." -- Deuteronomy 8:18

"Every man also to whom God hath given riches and wealth, and hath given him power to eat thereof, and to take his portion, and to rejoice in his labor – this is the gift of God." -- Ecclesiastes 5:19

Authoring my book was an arduous journey. There were so many moving parts. First, I needed to finish the writing and proofreading. Next, the manuscript was edited and then the book was formatted. Finally, the book went to the publisher. There was a moment or two that I considered keeping the books safe at home in a box. That was not really an option, but I got a bit nervous about having my feelings and emotions out there for anyone to read. I leaped and God met me in the gap. I have been able to minister to others who are dealing with losses. I have spoken to groups about trauma and loss; been featured as a guest on a podcast for caregivers. In these post-pandemic times, there are many people dealing with loss. I am still leaping as I walk into this new business—emerging as a sought-after speaker and strategist for people who are stuck in grief and stuck in life. I am still leaping as I nervously walk through the doors of opportunity that have opened since I wrote the book. Every challenge in my life has required me to leap, and every single time God has shown up in the gap with grace, access, and power.

Paula Anderson
www.livinonpurpose.com
palivinonpurpose@gmail.com

CHAPTER 19
YOUR CALLING IS YOUR PERMISSION

Change is inevitable. Whether you're looking to change your life with some drastic new beginning or just simply swapping out the kitchen paint color, for some of you, change of any kind can be a little daunting. As you know, by nature, we're creatures of habit, so it can take a little nudging to get us to make the leap of faith. Dr. Martin L. King, Jr. says, "Take the first step in faith, you don't have to see the whole staircase - just take the first step." At the young age of 22, I took my flip-flop wearing leap of faith into motherhood.

My life was Out-of-Control, just a whirlwind of NO parental guidance and looking for love in all the wrong boys to Men. Until I found myself, yet again, waiting for my name to be called at an abortion clinic. Jack Rabbits! I was just in this same dilemma five years ago. Now, I anxiously browse through old subscription magazines. In an attempt for conversation, my friend rattles on about this and that. I literally exhaled when she grabbed my hand, with tears in her eyes, and said, "You will make a great Mama." Half listening, half ignoring just the mention of 'mama' sent chills up my spine. What do I know about being a mother? Even though I made an awful lot of mistakes. It doesn't mean my life needs to be dull or mundane. It means that my life is full of possibilities.

I'm PREGNANT! How exciting to say these words. Most women think of creative ways to break the news to the father. For instance, a package that, when opened, reveals a disposable diaper with a baby bottle. Whatever the method, there's excitement and anticipation when this message of joy is shared. With that said, what if the thrill of discovering you are pregnant also brought havoc, disruption, and heartbreak to more than one relationship, because you are unable to recall the identity of the father? You can only imagine what went through my mind.

In Joshua chapter 2, we learn that two spies were sent to Jericho to look over the land, so this mission of espionage began. The spies went to the house of Rahab. They were still there when the King of Jericho sent his men looking for the spies. Rahab hid the spies on her roof and sent the King's men away. She committed treason! Then she had the nerve to ask the spies to spare her life in exchange for risking her life. Not only did this act save her life; it changed her heart. She is called 'righteous' in James 2:25. Her name is mentioned in the genealogy of Christ. I put aside being a woman who had numerous casual sexual encounters and turned to follow God.

On our way back to campus where I was pursuing a bachelor's degree in business administration, I actually just completed my freshman year. My friend struggled to console me, but I was overwhelmed by this new feeling called sober. Nothing stopped me from drinking until my drinking did. My mind was racing as I was trying to remember the pattern of the heartbeat I heard. Somehow, words that I couldn't even recognize as mine whispered, "I'm keeping my baby." If only I could turn back the hands of time, making sure I practiced safe sex. Shaking my head, no, today is a new day. This is the day I took a leap of faith, and I could feel it coming up from the very essence of my soul. I cleared my throat and with every ounce of courage I could muster, I screamed at the top of my lungs, "I'M KEEPING MY BABY!"

In November of 1991, my life was changed forever by waking up to my water-breaking in the intensive care unit (ICU). Imagine playing a game of baseball as a woman seven months pregnant and sliding into home plate to achieve a home run. Sounds so terrible, but it really wasn't. After five hours of intense labor with three long, out of breath pushes eventually able to exhale. Now, the nurse hands me this bundle of joy, which is when he finally lets out his "first" cry. "Is that how you greet your mama," I said. I remember the feeling of intense emotions. I had not seen a more beautiful face than his. I wanted to hold him close forever! As this nameless baby boy latches on for nursing; I simply lay back, close my eyes and whisper, "Lord, HELP ME?"

Perhaps you think of yourself without virtue. It may be that you haven't been the best example or have portions of your life of which you're not particularly proud. You may question, "How can I be an example of virtue to my child(ren), when I've been such a failure in so many ways. Rahab would certainly be considered a moral failure in today's society-I know I wouldn't be held up as an example of virtue. However, taking my cue from Rahab, I worked on changing my heart and lifestyle. In reality, we're soccer moms, businesswomen, and grandmothers with toddlers in tow. We have a diaper bag in one hand and a briefcase in the other. Children climb about our legs, while we discuss PTA meetings on the phone, stir dinner with one hand, and pull the dog off the table with the other.

The amazing news is that I'm speaking out about it; and willing to shed a little light at the end of the tunnel to give you comfort and motivation. One place that is a surefire source of encouragement toward growth is God's word. The Bible has so much to say on the goodness of change and God's presence is with you every step of the way. YES - It is challenging, at times, just remember God loves YOU! He gave his "only" son for you and me to have life. I did the same - give up my toxic and dysfunctional lifestyle, in order to better the odds against my son. It is not impossible to gather your faith and turn your children over to God in later years. You are His chosen steward for the children He has given you.

Taking a look at Luke 2:51-52, Jesus returned home with His mother and continued to obey her. It is stated by the Scriptures that from that time He increased in wisdom and structure, and in favor with God and men. He did not disassociate from His mother, whose loyalty followed Him all the way to the Cross. Although their roles changed and He became increasingly independent, His love and care for her continued even to His thirty-third year and the moments of His life. She was still His mother!

Most children have "I walked ten miles to school uphill in the snow without any shoes carrying both of my sisters on my back" stories. Being raised by a single mother, my child has shopping for shoes stories. In our public housing, Saturday mornings were known for one thing: riding the city bus to the shopping mall. Of course, he thought by curling his toes, I wouldn't purchase the off-brand shoes. My budget doesn't allow for all white Air Jordan. You probably have your own memories of childhood injustices. And you probably raised the same cry that my son did: "It's not fair!"

Like most parents, I responded along the lines of "Life's not fair," which is true. But recalling how Jesus handled a case of "injustice" in Luke 10:38. It's important to take my son's eyes away from the inequity and focus on the lesson. On my son's 31st birthday, I received my first pair of Air Jordan high-top shoes as a gift. What a privilege motherhood allows to produce a mannerable, educated, and no-baby daddy. I couldn't imagine going through life without feeling this spectrum of emotion. There were days that I wanted to run away and question every decision I have ever made. Feeling it all, good or bad, gives my life purpose.

As of 2017, in the role of Parent Life Coach, I commit my energy to ensure equity and create access to opportunities for young mothers of color. I inspire clients to switch from the role of diaper-changer, decision-maker, and discipline-enforcer to confidante, cheerleader, and champion. Motherhood is walking around with all of your nerve endings raw and exposed. It is the most extreme measure of being alive. As a black mother from a low-income community, it is a fulfillment of my purpose to ensure education and growth for the future of our children.

That is not promoting disrespect but development. If you respect yesterday's child and recognize that he has become today's adult, he will always love you for your tremendous contribution.

What about YOU? Are you ready to make some changes?

Rona Walton
www.RonaWalton.com
hello@ronawalton.com

CHAPTER 20
FEARFUL OF THE GAP

I was stranded on the edge of a cliff, holding on with bruised, bleeding, and swollen fingers. My feet were drenched with sweat from hours of straining and slipping repeatedly on the narrow edge. My back was pressed against the solid rock. It was a long way down from my forward-facing view of the canyon. My thought wasn't how I got there, but "What do I do now? I'm a long way from home and safety."

This was the horrible image in my head during my worst bout with anxiety. Every day, this image was in my mind. It was exactly how I felt. Any move could take me down instantly.

Recently the lender for my vehicle called to see when they could expect payment. I told him, "No time soon." After looking at my account for a few moments said, "You only have six payments left. Nobody defaults with only six payments to go! But you got a job!"

The job I had wasn't working out and I was out of money. It was 2008 and salesmen could sell jobs, but the banks wouldn't provide financing. Working commission only, with gas at $5 a gallon, I withdrew money from my investments to live on for a few weeks.

Losing your car is a big deal and I told my friends. Soon after, the guy I was dating pulled me aside. He said he had been gambling $400 every month and he wanted to stop. Thus, he would make the rest of my payments and that would stop him from gambling! He saw himself winning by making my car payments!

My darkness finally had some light and what a beautiful light it was. God sent me an angel that day!

Our relationship grew deeper, and we fell in love. Terry was struggling financially as well as working in construction and the Union had stopped calling.

The stones crunched under our feet as we walked to his black Chrysler 300. With no lead-up, Terry announced with enthusiasm and hope that he wanted to become a home inspector. Surprised, I stopped walking. He looked at me, and I at him. Next he asked if I would be his business partner. "Yes!" came out of my mouth as fast as lightning, and the dream of never working for an employer ever again suddenly became a beacon of hope in these desperate times.

We started a real estate consulting business at the same time as the mortgage crash. Persistence, determination, and the entrepreneurial dream pulled us through the beginning years. We relied on my sales and marketing skills to get our name out to the community. Terry provided the highest level of technical skill to set us apart from the competition.

It's been 14 years since we started our business and life is great now! We travel for both business and pleasure, we make our own schedule, we have a pontoon boat docked at our favorite lake, and we get to live out our why while doing the things we love to do. Years later I found out that Terry had been praying a very specific prayer to God for years. He would pray, "Lord, bring me a lady as crazy as me." God delivered in a big way!

But it wasn't always this way...

"Ask him to lunch," was followed by a gentle push on my right shoulder. My legs began to move. In my head I was scared, but I took four steps and spoke. "Do you want to go to lunch?" It wasn't an elaborate or clever invitation, but I did what my father asked.

I was standing on the deck of an indoor swimming pool near Philadelphia, PA. "He" was Tom, the father of my swimming student James.

Tom and I, along with James, met later at the restaurant in the country club. The conversation was pleasant but not memorable. Months later it led to a job opportunity with his company. The first year I was general office help, entrepreneurial assistant, and sounding board. The business had few clients and was struggling to sell to hotels and casinos. One day at lunch Tom told me we were launching a new product line, which he followed with, "And you are going to be the salesman!" with a broad smile across his face and jubilation in his voice.

Internally the next few seconds were long. "No, selling is my biggest fear! I can't do that!" In the next thought I jumped all in with, "Why not?" Then proudly, "It's my job now!" An unexpected pride filled my soul at that moment. I was in a new league. A league I had previously feared and never thought I would enter. God held my hand and jumped with me that day!

Opening doors and having interesting conversations with business owners was fun and came naturally. Then dedicating myself to learning sales to become a "Master Close" was a pursuit for years. Sales books, role-playing, storytelling, and learning from my peers' failures piloted me to the top of the field, earning bonuses and exotic trips.

During my B2B sales years, a long winter holiday at my parent's home was just what I needed to straighten out my head game. Until this point, I had very low self-esteem and was insecure about myself. While at home in Canton, Ohio, my mom and I went to the mall. My mom entered the Gap Clothing store while I stayed in the mall waiting for her to exit. After many minutes of waiting, I entered the store and experienced the worst feeling of displacement and inferiority I ever felt. "You don't belong in here" and "You're not worthy to be in the Gap" were my thoughts and feelings.

That experience hit me hard. I knew it was wrong. I knew it was an unresolved issue that I needed to address immediately to make a lasting and empowering change.

For an entire week, I sat in front of the fireplace and read the book *How to Win Friends and Influence People*. I took notes, studied the material, and journaled to help me organize my thoughts.

Eliminating the negative and focusing on the positive was the first change I made in myself. It was a constant struggle. My brain was programmed to think negative thoughts and it took a strong and consistent effort to make that change. Not only did I focus on eliminating negative thoughts about myself, but I also eliminated negative thoughts about others. I kept thinking, "Why am I allowing these negative thoughts to take up space in my brain when better stuff could be there?" Daily journaling is what cemented focusing on the positive in my life.

Foundational lessons were learned during this time. As I learned the lessons one by one, I wrote them down on the back of a business card. This card is well-worn because I kept it in the visor of my car and looked at it when needed, which was often. This card got me through many hard times when I was alone. My Black Belt Speaker Trainer Coach Jase Souder expressed that I have an "uncommon confidence" and the words to follow are the foundation for that confidence.

- I AM Beautiful
- I AM a GREAT Saleswoman
- ULTIMATE Confidence
- Eliminate the Negative, FOCUS on the POSITIVE
- What have I done for ME lately?
- ULTIMATE Persistence
- GIRL POWER
- EXCELLENT Presentation
- I'M GREAT! DON'T LET OTHERS BRING ME DOWN—ALWAYS!

While writing this chapter I wanted to find this card. I still had it but couldn't place it. After several failed search attempts, I stayed near the rooms my card could be within. The bedroom didn't have the right feeling, so I went back to my office where I sat down and said a little prayer, Then I performed a menial task until the Holy Spirit spoke; not actual words, but a sense to act. And when I did, I only moved one item in the drawer and there it was!

My years as a B2B saleswoman were formidable years and necessary to learn what I needed to know. I cherish those memories and life lessons learned.

Looking back, my greatest fear became my greatest gift. I've taught thousands of people sales skills, including my brother, who has mastered his craft. Sales were essential to be the woman God had planned for me.

That gentle push on my back all those years ago got me to where I am today. I was meant to be a saleswoman; I was meant to be a business owner. I was meant to plant seeds and sow them. I am a very blessed child of God and He will do the same for you. Jump into the gap and fall into His hands.

"Blessed is the one who perseveres under trial because, having stood the test, that person will receive the crown of life that the Lord has promised to those who love him." – James 1:12

Amy Kleptach
amy@tkhomeinspection.com
330.546.3765

CHAPTER 21
DREAMER ARISE

"Stand up, keep living!"

Somehow, I heard the voice calling me out of the heavy numbing state of broken dreams and despair that seemed to lull me into a certain state of sleep-filled lethargy.

The voice was faintly familiar as it seemed it was I, or at least the person I used to be, who was calling into a darkness that ragingly engulfed the heart that was losing its final reason to keep beating. It seemed, try as I may, my willpower had no power to deliver me.

With all my might, I wanted to heed the call. I wanted to come out of the deep sorrow that came like a thief in the middle of the night to steal my joy, my peace, and my very reason to live. I wanted with everything in me, to regain the vigor and zeal of the youthful woman who once stood in power and laughed at the future. Yet all my attempts proved futile. I could not shake the despair that filled my once-thriving soul. All the self-talk and guilt-ridden rebukes that I tossed like stones at my less-than-adequate self only managed to push me further away from the person I wanted to be.

I was truly lost.

I was dying with every breath I took.

There is nothing quite like the life-stealing hopelessness that smothers a once-burning ember and we wonder, will it ever live again?

Some may never know what could cause such deep brokenness or understand the force of an oppressive cloud given liberty to cast its shadow over the dream of a visionary. Pain and loss, disappointment and sorrow all play their part causing to fade the vision of the believer.

I do not know how I ended up in this unforgiving and unrelentless downhill spiral that seemed to have its destiny somewhere beneath the living, but I do know this.

It was there, amid the greatest darkness I ever knew, that I found this heart-wrenching Word to be true, "without a vision people perish." I lost sight of my future while gaining sight into this once-hidden mystery. As the days, weeks, and months seemed to endlessly appear, I felt powerless to end my plight as hope deferred and sorrow reigned.

For a dreamer, losing the ability to dream is devastating. For me, I was as the blind man who lost his sight. With the fleeing vision went the power of inspiration; the breath that gave me reason and purpose.

In this journey of understanding, such is true for the ones who can believe beyond what is tangible. As visionaries, we must look in the realm beyond the natural eye to see the battle that has been set in array against our hopes and our dreams. There we see the dream stealer himself. The one who is afraid to behold as faith invades and the dreamer takes a stand against all enemies that seek to darken the life of inspiration. We must be vigilant and dressed for battle as we stand ready to diligently fight for the purpose and destiny of our God-given dream.

Through this trial of faith, I have come to believe we have been created with a purpose that is innately impressed into our being as we were fashioned by the Creator himself. In this forming, there is a vision implanted deeply into the heart of every dreamer that the enemy wants us to abort but we are not unaware of his devices. Instead, in the face of adversity, we are led to embrace challenges that are sure to come as we understand trials and tribulations are designed to forge strength into the fibers of this masterpiece we are called to bring forth.

Friend, if you believe God has given you a dream, hold onto that dream as an invaluable treasure. As it comes forth it will be used to touch the lives of those around you.

Remember, the persistent dreamer will prevail and the one

who refuses to give up hope will walk in their vision and destiny. Looking back, I remember the moment everything began to change for me. I was living life on default. It was just another day of going through the motions as I hid my pain from those around me. After the day went on, I needed to hide away. The unbeckoned and familiar feelings of hopeless despair had come to overwhelm my soul once again.

The quiet darkened room at the end of the hall seemed to be my refuge. As I entered, I was quickly on the floor. It was as the weight of a thousand unspent tears seemed to drive me to my knees. I began to whisper a prayer as the many broken pieces tumbled out in tears before the Lord. Beyond asking for help, all I remember is whispering this prayer, "God, I have no reason to live. What am I to do?"

It was then I heard that still small voice. HIS voice. The one that breaks through dark places and shatters the deafening silence of muted hopes. My faith began to awaken. I knew when He speaks, darkness flees, and dead men come to life again.

His voice seemed to me as brief as an exhale and I was touched to the soul. It was as if He breathed life into my nostrils. I felt his voice deep within, as a rush of air sending quickening vibrations of hope to the dry bones and rekindling a soul growing in wavering faith.

I'll never forget the piercing touch of just a few simply spoken words that broke through the veil of my endless night, "What did you want to be?"

Suddenly He brought me back to when my dream was alive, and I was living a joyful life of expectancy.

I could hardly bring myself to answer the question that burned in my mind, yet I knew this was my moment for change. With a shaking and timid voice, I spoke into the air as I searched for a dream gone by. "I wanted to be a coach."

You see, for many years I had this reoccurring dream. I saw myself standing on stage and speaking into the lives of women who knew they were created with a God-given call to make an impact in the world. I knew I would be a voice declaring freedom to those in spiritual, financial, and physical bondage. No wonder the devil wanted to shut me down.

Within minutes I stood to my feet. The decision was made to begin impacting the lives of others through faith and business. I believed I could take my life and business experience to design a program that would fund my dream while helping others live theirs. I decided that day that I would start a coaching business. Within a couple of weeks, I found a coach that first aligned with my faith, and then what I needed to begin my business.

Here is the thing.

It took faith to leap behind the pile of ashes that had become my home.

It took faith to step into my dream before I really saw all the evidence of my healing. The truth is, I cried every single day for the first year of my business. I even cried on my coaching calls with my clients. The truth is at times I still cry, yet I show up and continue to take leaps of faith in the face of adversity. I refuse to quit! Such is the life of the believer; such is the life of the dreamer.

Friend, I know that stepping into your dream can be difficult. I understand the things that come and challenge your belief in the vision. I want to take a moment to empower you through words of hope and life.

If you believe God has given you a dream, then hold onto that dream through the pain of fire. Though there may come floods and high waters of adversity, I want to encourage you to have the mind to never give up. Rise up and stand in power. Stand for your dream even when you seem to be standing alone.

Step into action and begin living out your dream today. Let nothing hinder you, distract you or steal away your hope. My friend, it is time. Take the Leap of Faith and let the wings of inspiration propel you into your dream.

Jill Albanys
www.JillAlbanys.com
https://www.facebook.com/jill.albanys

CHAPTER 22
TAKING A LEAP OF FAITH

"Just take a Leap of Faith, trust God and it'll all be fine."
Sounds easy, right? But what happens when that Leap of Faith
requires you to walk away from everything you've ever been told
is good? You know, like climbing the corporate ladder, getting a
raise, building a retirement account, making a name for yourself
and having greater influence?

And what do you do when the one calling you to take a Leap
of Faith is God himself?

I want to take you back for a minute and share with you my
first Leap of Faith. I was working as the Women's Health Clinical
Nurse Educator for a small, rural hospital that I'd worked at for 15
years. When I went to work that morning, it was supposed to be
just another routine day. But by the time I went home that
afternoon, my entire life would have changed.

It was nearing the end of the day when my manager came to
my office. This 'drop-in' was pretty normal as we both had an
open-door policy and often would pop into each other's offices just
to say 'hi', see how our families were, what the weekend plans
were.

She had such a big heart and loved her 'work family' almost
to a fault. As she came through my door that day her entire
beingness was different... the hesitancy in her approach was
palpable. As she sat down in the chair, she said something so
strange. She said, "Natalie, I have something I want to talk to you
about and I hope you'll accept my offer." I wasn't quite sure what
to do with that statement but listened as she continued. It turned
out I'd just been given the opportunity to move into a
management position. I can remember being so excited, but also a

little confused because I had anticipated another 2-3 years before I had that opportunity. Nevertheless, I was one step closer to a dream I had set my sights on years ago and I felt like I had finally achieved success.

And yet - something still felt off about it.

Since it was Friday and we were about to head to the lake (my happy place) for the weekend, I had plenty of time to consider the offer that was on the table. And in that time away, God began whispering to my heart; showing me things that I hadn't considered and people who would also be affected by this decision. And I began to question if this really was the dream I had hoped for. I mean, it was great for me - great for my career - but I began to realize it might not be so great for my young family. You see, I had three little boys (only three, six, and nine years old) at the time. I already had to endure the look of sadness on their faces as I left each morning, and sometimes at night, or on the weekend, for work. They didn't understand bills and mortgages and things of the 'adult' world. All they knew was mommy had to leave - again.

And all they wanted and needed was their momma, to be home with them, to teach them, train them, play with them, and show them how to become Godly men. My heart began to break. I realized I would be giving that up if I took this promotion, because I would be working all week and on call 24/7. I could see their little tear-stained faces as I left - missing out, not only on some of the most important once-in-a-lifetime moments of their lives, but on the everyday, simple moments that would shape their future. And for what? The 'All-American Dream'? Being able to "measure up" in the 'who's-who' of the corporate world? It was a house of cards - and it was crumbling.

So, where do you go from a moment like that? What do you do when the thing you've been dreaming of and working so hard for, is now within your grasp and you realize, it's not a dream you even want anymore?

Well, get ready because this is where the plot gets even thicker.

While I was being offered this promotion, we simultaneously experienced administrative turnover at the executive leadership level of our organization. Our new executive team determined the Clinical Nurse Educator role was no longer needed and was going to be eliminated. Yep, you heard me right - ELIMINATED. Talk about feeling like you're hit by a ton of bricks! Feeling the impact of the 'opportunity' on my family was the first blow, but now this! The pressure I felt was crushing. I couldn't breathe... it felt like I was being buried under a ton of bricks! If I turned this promotion down... I was ending my career. No pay raise. No retirement. No further contribution to my profession. And worse yet... my family. How would I provide for them? Keep them fed? Would we lose our house? Would my marriage crumble under the financial pressure?

Breathe...

'Ok, now what God?' I could barely get the words out around the crushing pressure I felt in my chest. 'Now what am I supposed to do?'

His reply, "Follow me."

'Follow you'—where? I live 30 miles from any hospitals, and any job I would find at one would be a massive step backward for my career and finances.

"Start your own business," He said.

"My own business? I don't know how to start a business." I said.

"Yes, you do. You did it with the lactation program at the hospital. You did it when you helped start the School of Nursing. You can do it again for yourself with my help." He replied.

I had no idea at the time how it was going to work out, all I knew was I wanted to obey God and I wanted to be there for my kids. So, I turned down the promotion, cleaned out my office, and took a giant leap of faith into the deep unknown.

And if I'm honest, when I look back, I had been craving the deep unknown, where the things of God are, for quite some time and just didn't realize it.

Well, it wasn't long before finances started getting tight. My husband and I weren't sure how we were going to make the next mortgage payment. I started thinking, 'Is this it, God? Have we come this far only to fail?'. (Sound familiar? Just like the people of Israel I told you about at the beginning of this book.) Just as we were about out of time and out of money, one day the phone rang. I answered. The woman on the other end proceeded to tell me that an error had been made on our taxes a couple of years ago and we would be receiving a check in the mail for $5,000.00!

"Thank you, God!" I said as tears of relief welled up in my eyes.

Not long after that I found a job at a hospital that was about an hour and a half away, but where I could do work I liked, make more money per hour than I did at the job I just left and work as much or as little as I wanted—giving me time to continue growing my business.

"Thank you again, God." It was His provision in the process at play.

I continued working jobs 'as needed' until my business was making enough money to support itself and start paying me. And then I took the Leap of Faith into full time entrepreneurship.

It's been six and a half years now since taking that first Leap of Faith and God has been there with me every step of the way. Entrepreneurship has become a journey of faith rather than a leap. Every day takes me a few steps further down the path and my relationship with God gets deeper and deeper.

I wish I could tell you it gets easier—it doesn't. The greater the success, the greater the Leaps of Faith required to keep going. And truthfully, it's in the 'hard' that the priceless moments of closeness with God happen. It's where your faith grows deeper and stronger, and you get to experience knowing that there truly are no words to describe. So, in a way, I actually don't wish it to be easy for you. I want you to experience for yourself the sweetness and richness of His love and provision. I want you to be willing to take that Leap of Faith time and time again because you now know, beyond the shadow of a doubt, that God will always be standing in the gap for you.

Natalie Lavelock
www.NatalieLavelock.com
Natalie@NatalieLavelock.com

THANK YOU!

Thank you so much for taking the time to read *Leap of Faith*. I hope it leaves you feeling deeply inspired, encouraged, and motivated to step into your calling and take your own leap.

Would you take just a moment and leave a review on the book page? It would mean the world! This is one of the ways you can help get this book into more hands.

Share here: *amazon.com/dp/B0CJQ1KLF5*